TALKING TO STAKEHOLDERS

COPYRIGHT © 2025 ALEXANDRA MACK

All rights reserved. This book or parts thereof may not be reproduced in any form, stored in any retrieval system, or transmitted in any form by any means—electronic, mechanical, photocopy, recording, or otherwise—without prior written permission of the publisher, except as provided by United States of America copyright law.

ISBNs:	eBook	978-1-944627-20-1
	Paperback	978-1-944627-21-8

By reading this document, the reader agrees that under no circumstances is the author or the publisher responsible for any losses, direct or indirect, which are incurred as a result of the use of information contained within this document, including, but not limited to, errors, omissions, or inaccuracies.

LEGAL NOTICE:

This book is copyright protected. Please note the information contained within this document is for educational and personal use only. You cannot amend, distribute, sell, use, quote, or paraphrase any part, or the content within this book, without the consent of the author or publisher.

TALKING TO STAKEHOLDERS

How to Add Value and Make an Impact by Building Strategic Relationships

ALEXANDRA MACK

Praise for *Talking with Stakeholders*

"To succeed in our world, to be promoted, and to get your ideas heard, you have to reframe your work so it matters to your stakeholder—and that means listening to them. With many relatable stories and examples, Mack breaks down some of the trickiest parts of that process."
—BRUCE MCCARTHY, Founder, Product Culture and co-author of *Aligned: Stakeholder Management for Product Leaders*

"We've finally realized that building relationships with our stakeholders is the key to helping make a difference for people in our work. And relationships are about deep listening, embracing new perspectives, and supporting those perspectives. Alex Mack's book helps us see where to change our approaches so that we can support our stakeholders in ways they need—and to communicate the knowledge they are able to make decisions with. Make them feel heard."
—INDI YOUNG, Research Expert, author of *Time to Listen*

"I read *Talking to Stakeholders* at a point in my career where I should know how to talk to stakeholder, yet this book showed me quite a thing or two. It's an excellent refresher for those that are experienced, an approachable primer for those just learning, and a must read for anyone wanting to level up their skills. Using decades of corporate and lived human experience, Mack distills the core of good stakeholders relationship building down for you in a concise read: be curious and remove your ego!"
—LAURYL ZENOBI, Director of Digital Services at Vaultes

"Functional expertise is table stakes—consulting skills are what will set you apart. *Talking to Stakeholders* delivers practical moves to accelerate your journey to becoming a trusted professional. Instead of learning the hard way, Mack equips you to communicate with, align, and influence stakeholders with confidence, driving meaningful impact in every initiative you lead."
—ROBIN BEERS, PhD, Organizational Psychologist

"Alex has written something remarkable here: a book helping everyone who has to deal with stakeholders, which is to say everyone, deal with them better. Whether you're an engineer, a product manager, a designer, or just someone who wants to get things done, this book will help you understand your stakeholders, talk to them more effectively, and make them allies instead of adversaries."
—CARTER BAXTER, Consulting Engineer & Management Consultant

"For those of us who believe that 'soft skills' should in fact be called 'core skills,' this book meets a real need. Many hard working and highly capable people nevertheless fail to make an impact on their organizations and build the careers they want. Alexandra Mack shows how to avoid this: by arriving at a better understanding of the broader business context, by mapping the stakeholder landscape, and by getting better at communicating with the people who have influence over your work. Perhaps most importantly, each chapter is practical and actionable; no one becomes massively influential overnight, but this book outlines the things you can do every day to earn respect and become vastly more effective over time."
—KATE WALTON, Owner, Steyer Content

To all my stakeholders

CONTENTS

Introduction — 1

Chapter 1. Who Are Your Stakeholders? — 11

Chapter 2. Understanding the Big Picture — 31

Chapter 3. Listening to Your Stakeholders — 51

Chapter 4. Helping with Your Stakeholders' Problems — 75

Chapter 5. Saying No Without Saying No — 93

Chapter 6. Presenting Your Work Effectively — 119

Chapter 7. When Stakeholders Are Difficult — 135

Conclusion — 157

Acknowledgements — 167

INTRODUCTION

Years ago, one of my colleagues at Pitney Bowes was complaining to me. "They never listen to me! I work really hard and my work never moves forward! The product team just sits there and listens and then they do nothing."

I had worked with this colleague for two years at this point. I knew she did excellent work, with a good eye for technical detail. She functioned as team lead well, and the research itself was good. However, she was frustrated, just like many technical specialists in a variety of fields are frustrated. How can you do good work and that work go nowhere? How can you make more impact when no one seems to listen to you?

At my colleague's request, I sat in on her presentation of her team's findings. They had been tasked with researching what the users wanted and needed from the product. Unfortunately, she presented their findings in the worst way possible for a business audience. She began with the methodology in detail and continued to present all of their findings, piece by piece. The presentation was twice as long as it needed to be, and she never recommended anything concrete to make the product better.

Her manager sighed before the end and did not ask her to present her findings to the client. Later that month, my colleague was passed over for a promotion.

I've seen this dynamic many times, not just with researchers, but also software developers, data scientists, and technical writers. I've heard about it in other fields, with aerospace engineers, architects, and up-and-coming lawyers. Good work alone is not enough. Even excellent work paired with ambition can leave you speaking into the void.

Maybe you've been there. You gave your client presentation, and they seemed to like what you had to say and agreed with you. Yet they don't seem to act on the information you've given them. You're left wondering why. Your manager passes on your work and praises you on a technical level, but your career goes nowhere. You're confused and frustrated.

Fortunately, the invisible barrier you're facing is real, and it can be overcome.

The Next Level

Becoming excellent at your craft is necessary and will earn you recognition—up to a point. Reaching the next level then becomes about other things, including managing people, balancing budgets, keeping track of complex projects, and maintaining timelines. People will naturally identify and address many of these missing skills as they become more senior, but some skills prove more difficult to address. For most people I've seen who continue to struggle, they're missing one skill in particular: talking to stakeholders.

The truth is that no one teaches talking to stakeholders. However, it's a critical skill; if you do it well, you will unstick or dramatically accelerate your career growth. You'll obtain more business, referrals, and renewals for your organization and make your projects more successful. You will build more of the right thing at the right time in the right way, making your work exponentially more valuable to your organization and your clients alike. All of this will make it easier to build a great network and to find your next opportunity.

The long-standing tale of the self-made career person is a myth. None of us make it entirely on our own,[1] and while peers can help you, the people with the most power to help or hinder you are, by definition, stakeholders.[2] They can support you in your projects, your career, and your work or become an active impediment. They can hire and fire you. Even if you become self-employed at some point, you will still need to talk to stakeholders (clients and others) to be successful. In the corporate world, your career literally cannot progress past a certain point without someone above you actively supporting it. Talking to stakeholders is critical.

Earning More Impact

Many technical specialists have the belief that doing good work should be enough on its own, but this belief is erroneous. For better or worse, all of our work only matters if people see why and how it is important. A simple painting without a frame covered in dust at a flea market will appear far less valuable than the same painting richly framed behind glass at an art museum. The context gives the work its value, but the context can be changed.

Talking to stakeholders well means learning to place your work in the right frame so that they can understand and value that work. It means deliberately building the type of relationships with stakeholders that lead to mutual respect so that they will listen to your recommendations or even seek out your opinion.

When you can put yourself in the shoes of your stakeholder, understand deeply what is important to them, and do the work

---

1 Of course, I realize that we as a society put the lone abrasive genius on a pedestal, holding up Steve Jobs in his day as uniquely successful, but they are the exceptions. Generally work is very much a team sport.

2 There are many definitions of stakeholders, but in this book, we define them as people with the power to help or hurt your work directly. Typical stakeholders include bosses, clients, executives, and anyone with the power to influence outcomes, even if informally.

of connecting what you have to what they care about, you earn more impact. You also become far more valuable.

Talking Can Be Learned

In 2002, when I worked at a consultancy, there was a recession. The very small company had to do layoffs, twice. The first time, they made a mistake, calling three of us into the office and assuring us that we were safe due to the quality of our work. "You are our top people." This helped us feel secure, despite the challenges of knowing our friends and colleagues were out of work.

Time went on, the recession got worse, and the situation changed. The company was forced to do another round of layoffs. One of the three people who were brought into the office was let go, and she was justifiably upset. (Incidentally, this is why you should never promise anyone is safe; circumstances may force you to betray your promise and lead to far more distress for everyone.)

With the second round of cuts, they told us that while the woman had been a truly amazing designer, she was also abrasive when she spoke to stakeholders. When they were getting down to a skeleton staff, they realized that her skills did not outweigh the abrasiveness. Soft skills do matter.

I have seen people who are extraordinary at what they do torpedo their careers through a few badly thought out interactions with stakeholders. Others who are nearly as good never get the hang of the skills involved in talking to stakeholders, and it prevents their ideas from being heard and their work from being acted on. I have even seen people who are not technical stand-outs advance their careers much faster than their peers by employing these sets of skills. Talking to stakeholders is absolutely a crucial skill, and it's something you can learn.

Talking to Stakeholders

In this book, I will walk you through the essentials involved in talking to stakeholders, but the essence is simple. You will put yourself in the shoes of your stakeholder, understand deeply what is important to them, and do the work of connecting what you have to what they care about.

Talking to stakeholders is often about who is doing the work. Are you making them do the work to connect your ideas to their reality and to understand why your input is valuable? (They may or may not be able to do this work given the other demands on their schedule.) Or, do you go the extra mile to connect your ideas to their reality? If you frame your technical insights so that the connection is already clear, the stakeholder can own it and run with it immediately.

The people who earn influence for their work are the ones who understand how to frame that work for the most impact and do so consistently.

My Experience

Perhaps it's not surprising that talking to stakeholders is difficult. In many circumstances, we are actively taught other ways of approaching people. Before I worked in corporate America, I came up through academia. Behaviors that are very standard in academia to prove your case and show your authority turned out to be counterproductive when I moved into industry.

For example, starting with methodology and including every detail, as my colleague did in the story that starts this introduction, is a powerful authority builder in academia. Academia teaches you to *prove* your case and to do so in an argumentative fashion. You are taught to focus on being right and/or proving others wrong. Unfortunately, this approach is counterproductive in business. Making your stakeholders feel wrong will operate as a strike against you, and getting them to "right" is most effective when done gently. In fact, in the ideal situation, your stakeholders should come to see the "right" idea as theirs.

I made many mistakes when transitioning from academia to industry and government spaces, but I learned steadily from those mistakes. To survive and thrive, I slowly began to communicate at the level that stakeholders expected, within the frameworks they understood. While I will stand by my work as strongly now as I did in academia, my approach to communication has changed dramatically.

Over the last two decades, I've spoken with stakeholders successfully in a wide variety of situations and industries. As one of the first anthropologists they hired, I helped establish the new research and analysis program at Pitney Bowes. I have worked on projects across a variety of industries, including health care, retail, software, government, nonprofit, and financial services. I have also served on the executive board of several nonprofits and advised faculty entrepreneurs through Yale Ventures. At the time of this writing, I am the current Director of Research at Ad Hoc LLC, working with teams of researchers, designers, engineers, and product managers building digital services for government clients.

Across all of this experience and all of these industries, I have found talking to stakeholders to be *the* skill that no one teaches, and the skill that my teams most need. And since I had to learn it the hard way, I found that I was uniquely able to teach the people who came to me for help.

Learning this skill has made an immense difference in the work and careers of the people I mentor. I have presented these ideas in talks and classes with positive responses and requests to speak more widely. This interest has led me to want to offer a resource to the community at large. Talking to stakeholders seems to be one of those things that you are simply expected to figure out, but so many people struggle to do so. I feel strongly that it's time for the community to have resources on learning it, and this book is the result.

What You'll Learn

This is intended as a practical but not a prescriptive book. In these pages I will explain what works and what doesn't in talking to stakeholders across a variety of fields, with examples where possible. The book is written specifically with technical practitioners in mind, though it may also be useful for managers or more general businesspeople, depending on circumstance. The core is still most useful for technical practitioners already excellent in their field.

In this book, I'll cover how to:

- Talk so stakeholders will listen
- Make effective stakeholder presentations
- Discover (and deliver) the true goals of your stakeholders
- Manage situations in which you and your stakeholders are not on the same page
- Deal with that one difficult stakeholder

Along the way, I'll explain principles and give examples and scripts where needed. Many of my examples will come from my background and experience, along with (anonymized) stories from a variety of colleagues past and present. My examples will lean toward research, design, and product development, but the principles remain applicable across specialties.

Since I believe in assumption mapping, I will further detail my assumptions here. I assume that you are already excellent in your specific set of technical skills, whatever they are, or that you are working diligently to become so. I also assume you are working with stakeholders on a regular basis or that you have enough experience in your organization to have done so in the past. So while you *could* use this book to improve interactions with your boss alone, that's not its primary purpose.

I also assume that you are familiar with and competent in basic people skills or know that you are not; if the latter, I suggest you seek out a book on people skills, of which there are many, and read and study that one before coming back to this book. The advanced skills here will be greatly strengthened by your having already mastered the basic ones.

How to Get More Out of This Book

Each of the seven chapters in this book builds on the last, so you will get the most out of the book if you read it through at least once as a whole, rather than jumping around. You will also get more value if you read the book with a problem or situation in mind. At the end of each chapter, I will encourage you to do an exercise. Applying that exercise to your problem or situation will help you learn application of the general principles in a deeper way. You may also find it helpful to come back and reread important chapters as new situations come up.

Like any craft, talking to stakeholders can't be entirely learned from a book, regardless of how carefully you study. Just like learning a new part of your technical specialty, learning this may feel awkward at first, but if you persist, your confidence and abilities will grow. Be aware that, since talking to stakeholders is a *complex* skill, it will take time to master all the dependent pieces and to integrate them together. You may need several tries to be able to successfully apply a general principle to a specific situation or to learn to dial in the right approach without it feeling awkward and unnatural. The good news is that the difficulty is directly proportional to the payoff; if you persist, you'll see your projects and your career improve in ways that your less-skilled peers may not.

And lastly, as you already know from your own technical specialty, advanced practice of a craft requires judgment. While the general approach to all situations may be remarkably similar, each situation is different. As such, this guide to talking to stakeholders cannot be a step-by-step algorithm. Rather, it is a framework, and one that will require adapting to your style and situation. Try the techniques, learn them, and apply them to your circumstances. Once you know and can practice the principles, make them yours, and break them for good reasons when the situation requires it. Where I provide a script, change the words to make them yours.

For your interactions with stakeholders to come across as authentic, you *must* act in a way that is true to yourself and your personality. Experiment, learn, and then make these techniques your own.

CHAPTER ONE

WHO ARE YOUR STAKEHOLDERS?

Stakeholders are critical to the success of your career, but there are more of them beyond just your boss and your clients. Each stakeholder is also an individual, a person, with their own needs and values.

EARLY IN MY CAREER AT A CONSULTING COMPANY, I HANDLED A situation with a stakeholder poorly. The client was accompanying me on contextual interviews, a mode of research where you observe someone doing their work and ask them questions for clarification. If you cannot actively observe the person approaching the task or tool in real time, there are specific techniques you can use to get them to recall a past instance of the work and to describe it in more detail. My boss at the time was insistent on following an exact process.

One participant, a lower-level executive, was not doing the task in real time. So, I asked him to recall a specific instance, and he answered my questions in broad generalities. I responded as my training told me to do, by pushing the executive to be specific. I asked questions like, "When was the last time you did this?" and "Can you walk me through what you did?" He responded again with generalities, I responded again with a request for specifics, and the pattern repeated.

Unfortunately, the client felt that I was pestering their important executive-level customer rather than respecting his expertise. The client stepped in and took over the conversation. Later, he complained to my boss.

Now, to this day I do not know if the executive was bothered by me insisting on specifics, but the client absolutely was. My stakeholder there was the client, and I was not nearly power sensitive enough or deferential enough in speaking to their customer for their liking. I was doing what my boss had told me to do, but that didn't matter. My boss did not defend me for following the process, instead scolding me.

The work of running a successful career or project is often balancing the input and influence of a variety of people. I made my mistake by not being sensitive to power and to context. If instead I had recognized *all* of my stakeholders in the situation, I could have been more responsive to context.

Before you can interact well with stakeholders, you must first be able to identify all the ones who may influence your immediate situation. Over the years, I've found that stakeholders include both the "important" and obvious ones with formal power *and* the ones with informal power or influence who may not be obvious at first glance.

Stakeholders Are People with Power or Influence

Especially in complex organizations, power and influence are never completely reflected in the org chart. I can't tell you how many times I've seen someone outside the reporting structure have the influence to change an important part of the project at the last minute. While not every indirect stakeholder wields this much power, it is nonetheless important to understand the influence they do have.

For instance, a classic example of indirect influence is the CEO's golf buddy, who may be relatively junior, with no formal power, but whose words can often have an outsized impact on the CEO's decisions. I learned in graduate school to make nice with the department secretary because she could help me set up meetings and get access to resources I desperately needed to succeed. Executive assistants control access to people with power. While they may not in theory have a vested interest in your project, if they can block it, their goodwill matters greatly to its success.

This leads to our definition. A stakeholder is not just the decision maker for your project or anyone who directly influences him or her but also anyone with a vested interest in the outcome of a project *and* who has the power to help or hinder it. That definition includes decision makers, secondary decision makers, and also influencers, such as the executive assistant or your CEO's golf buddy. **Anyone who has a large enough voice to affect the outcome is a stakeholder.**

This definition of stakeholder includes less visible people in the organization who may be affected by your project. For example, if you're running a project for a software organization, whoever runs the call center may have a vested interest in changes to your software product. He or she oversees people who will get customer service calls if the UX is poor. If he or she can dramatically affect the project by saying, "This thing is gonna upset the work of the call center," the manager is a stakeholder. He or she speaks with a loud voice in the organization, and people listen.

In some organizations, people like that call center manager, with a vested interest in the outcome of the project, aren't treated as stakeholders internally. However, if they become frustrated, they can sometimes make themselves heard late in the game.

Sometimes those late-breaking voices can be more impactful (and sometimes more disruptive) than any waves made by people with formal power. You can't always tell from the outside whether someone has influence or not, so I recommend taking the time to identify those people who may want to make themselves heard *before* major work happens. You will want to ensure they are allies and not enemies to your efforts.

Talking with stakeholders *well* is about more than just having good conversations and requires talking to more people than just your boss and clients. I recommend understanding your entire ecosystem of stakeholders so that you know who can affect your outcomes and spending the time to know them and build relationships with them so that they become your allies.

In this chapter, I will help you identify who *all* of your stakeholders are, which is always the first step in talking to them successfully.

Not Everyone Is a Stakeholder

Stakeholders are (1) *internal* to your or your client's or a partner organization, with both (2) a *vested interest* and (3) the *power or influence* to ensure that interest is addressed. While it may seem pedantic to point out, anyone who does not have all three aspects is not a stakeholder.

Many practitioners claim that users are stakeholders or that the community they are serving is a stakeholder, but that is not how I use the term. While the community, users, or consumers may have a vested interest in the outcome of a project, they do not have any direct *influence* on it or the *power* to help or hinder that outcome in any particular direction. They are also outside your organization and outside your client's organization, which excludes them. A single representative of a community advocacy organization with the mayor's ear, in contrast, may or may not operate as an influencing stakeholder if you are working closely with the mayor on a project. Stakeholders are also not ordinarily your peers. While coworkers could help you along or hinder your progress, they don't have the direct power or influence that the term *stakeholder* implies. Stakeholders are decision makers and the peripheral people with influence over those decision makers, not including yourself. They are assumed to be internal to your organization or a client or associated organization that you are working with directly.

Common Stakeholder Types

I have worked in companies where all of the stakeholders are internal to the organization that was writing my paycheck. I have also worked with companies in which other parties in other organizations, for whatever reason, are also extremely important to the success of any given project. Whether within your organization or not, however, stakeholders tend to fall into common types.

Common stakeholders within your organization often include:

- Your supervisor
- Your supervisor's boss
- Product owners
- Executives
- Other decision makers
- Interested parties in other departments who can influence or hinder your project
- Gatekeepers, such as the executive assistant to a decision maker
- Other notable influencers within your organization

Common stakeholders outside your organization often include:

- The people at the client or partner organizations you interact with
- Those peoples' bosses and influencers
- Outside experts whose opinion is respected

Each of these stakeholders may be working in a very different type of environment. Your knowledge of them may also vary.

Decision Making Is Not Always Straightforward

In some organizational realities and consulting situations, it can be hard to put a finger on exactly who the decision maker is. The thing that you are working on may be complex or sit between departments. At other times, the way that decisions are made becomes necessarily complex. In the government environment, that is particularly true.

If you cannot identify your decision maker precisely, move forward by identifying who *needs* to be on your side for the project to be successful. Then treat those people as your power players, or primary stakeholders, whether or not they actually make decisions. When a conflict comes up, try to get *all* of the affected stakeholders in the room. Only when the situation cannot be resolved to everyone's liking should you make decisions based on position.

Building Allies Within Limitations

In a perfect world, it would be possible to fully understand the influencers and power players of any given system of stakeholders and to talk to and make allies with all of them. Unfortunately, we do not live in a perfect world. If you work in certain types of consulting with three-month projects, you will never get a full understanding in that time frame. You may be able to map your own organization with a high degree of accuracy, even to the level of informal influence, for example, but find similar knowledge hard to find in a partner organization, even on a longer timescale.

No matter how carefully you try, you will never be able to talk to every stakeholder with power or influence on your project. Time is a meaningful limitation and so are organizational dynamics. Some powerful people you will simply never get to. Their influence will also matter, and you may want to equip those who *can* talk to them to do so better if you can.

That being said, you will want to find and to reach out to as many stakeholders as possible within your time frame to build your base of allies. I recommend consciously prioritizing anyone who *needs* to be on your side for the project to move forward. Anyone who *must* buy in should come first. To return to the example of the manager of the call center, if he or she can cause a fuss that will shut down the project or change its scope or features at the last minute, that person should be consulted early. A good working relationship with them strongly ensures success. His or her executive assistant, on the other hand, may or may not be as critical to consult immediately, though they should be treated well at all times.

Systems and Ecosystems

Stakeholders operate within a larger ecosystem. This stakeholder ecosystem is the overall set of people with different roles, power, and influences who interact. Each individual stakeholder may talk to others. One person's actions and opinions can have ripple effects across the system.

If you are not familiar with systems theory, a *system* is a group of discrete parts that have to be considered as a whole. For example, our physical bodies are systems. So while it is common to have doctors who specialize in skin, or hearts, or lungs, an issue that affects one part of the body is frequently caused by and dependent on the issues of other parts. Doctors who become undulyfocused on their part of the system without considering the rest of the body can often miss important information and misdiagnose. They can treat symptoms without actually finding the underlying disease.

When looking at your stakeholders and who has power and influence, also consider the system in which they operate within your organization. How does one person's actions influence the rest? How does larger-scale communication affect the system?

You may also need to consider more than one system and their interactions. For example, my current organization has several discrete business units. We do software work for several government organizations working with prime contractors and subcontractors. In this space, projects tend to operate in *ecosystems,* or multiple overlapping systems of stakeholders among many different organizational systems. Your situation is unlikely to be as complex as this one, where we have to please both our prime contractors and the government agencies they support, for example, but it's worth mentioning how deeply complex stakeholder ecosystems can get.

For an easier example of stakeholder ecosystems, I'll discuss a friend's experience. She is leading a small consultant team providing services to a large client organization in manufacturing and doing a good job of addressing the primary decision maker's needs within that client organization. Unfortunately, due to the internal politics of the client organization, the person who is supposed to be the decision maker, who we'll call Andrew, is being overshadowed by another party of similar rank, Brad, and a difficult secondary influencer Catherine.

As my friend put it, she will go to Andrew and get his buy-in, and everything seems great. Then she'll go back to Andrew two weeks later, and Brad has gotten in the middle and effectively overridden Andrew's decision within the larger organization. Then later, after Andrew and Brad have talked with outside influencer Catherine, suddenly the tune has changed. In the meeting, my friend will talk about the decision, and—as she puts it—Andrew will crumble.

The challenging nature of the stakeholders my friend is coping with have, in practice, nothing to do with the org chart. Neither Brad nor Catherine should be making decisions, but the organizational dynamics are such that what they say carries weight beyond their role. As such, my friend must shift to also including them and addressing their concerns.

There will be personalities and relationships and power plays that your team must figure out based on limited information and negotiate appropriately to get the work done. In my current company's case, we must sometimes identify stakeholders in the prime organization, the government agency organization, and across different business units in our own organization. In all cases, there will be people with formal and informal power and influence who need to be accounted for.

Identifying the complexities early may not prevent difficult situations from arising, but it will make it easier to negotiate them. Do the work to identify your stakeholders, and do not blithely assume that the org chart will tell you everything you need to know. You will need to remain open to additional information as it comes up and be ever-cognizant of informal structures which may drive decision making in practice.

Another Example of a Stakeholder Ecosystem

I will give you one additional example from my time at Pitney Bowes. At the time, they were building their first software as a service (SaaS) product, which was a significant move for this previously hardware-based company. They had hired an international design firm to design their customer experience, but the budget wasn't there to continue to pay that firm. The General Manager of the product tasked me with the end-to-end customer experience after the initial design was complete. I worked with him to identify key experiences for customers in the product that we needed to be successful, including in-app help.

This experience would *not* work without the active help and participation of several departments, including UX, engineering, IT, and the web team. It was a classic case of responsibility without authority; I had to corral people from different silos together to jury-rig something good enough to be released.

At one point, I had a stakeholder say to me, "I understand what you're trying to do, and this makes sense, but that's not in my objectives." Everyone had different goals, and all of those goals were reasonable, but none of them aligned together. Yet my success depended on working across silos and winning the help of various stakeholders despite their opposing goals on paper.

The project would have been impossible if I had not used the skills I will teach you in the rest of this book. The first step was identifying the power players and influencers, mapping as much of the ecosystem of stakeholders as possible, and determining what each person as an individual and each part of the system needed to move forward. Then it was a matter of building relationships to get what I needed.

In some cases, people literally would not agree to help, and in those cases, I had to find another way to the goal. For example, when I could *not* get the help of a content specialist from one team, we got a technical writer from a different part of the organization. Even here, knowing the ecosystem was profoundly helpful in charting a different path to get what I needed. I built relationships and earned influence deliberately, and that influence allowed me to find workarounds to get the experience launched.

The Stakeholders You Do Not See

Be aware, there will inevitably be a stakeholder essential to the success of your project that you cannot directly see. For example, in the case of the complex government space, you may work with a client every day who cannot make key decisions themselves. You can present to your client's boss, but you won't be able to even get in a room with their boss's boss, no matter how well you maneuver the situation.

I've faced many situations where the actual decision-making power lies with a stakeholder I cannot interact with directly. In those cases, I work with the immediate representatives to help them make the case to their boss about the work we do.

Particularly in government, politics can become an interesting influence on what happens in the day-to-day work. A person in power may dictate something, it filters down, and you may have to do it without asking questions. If someone calls their senator about something, and the senator calls the agency, for example, that may result in a high-priority change.

Sometimes the only choice is to influence the people you don't see through the people you do. You must also learn to be alert for things that may happen within the agency that you don't have control over and trust your instincts as to when to push back and when not to. In some circumstances, I've created detailed slide decks and presentations to help my immediate stakeholder make the case for why a specific policy change may sabotage another agency priority, for example. In other times, I've made the change requested without complaint. In both circumstances, I've built a strong enough relationship with both my immediate and other stakeholders that I had a clear idea of what would and would not be helpful.

Stakeholders Are People

When it comes to large bureaucracies and complex systems, my mentees like to say, "The agency says this," or, "Accounting has this policy." My response is always, "Yes, but *who?*" No organization makes a decision. *People* within the organization make decisions, even if those decisions are made in groups or influenced by many competing factors. Understanding the organization's values and issues (as I discuss in the next chapter) will be of immense help, but it's not enough if you don't also understand your stakeholders' specific motivations. Even if someone you can't see made that decision, it was a person, or a set of people, and people can change their minds.

No matter how unilateral and forbidding the decision feels, focusing on the *people* is ultimately empowering. You can introduce yourself to people and build relationships with people. You can earn influence with individual people and understand their hopes, fears, and motivations in ways that you can't with a faceless organization. To make any change at all or to create lasting successful projects, you do so by getting to know people and building good relationships with those stakeholders who most matter.

When a decision comes down that isn't ideal for a project, my first question is, who? That answer will help you determine what you do about the decision and what workarounds might exist. What are the ultimate goals of this person? What else can you do to accomplish those goals? Where does the concern come from? Even difficult information will teach you more about the landscape, headwinds, and the complexity of the system. In contrast, if you say, "Accounting decided," that sentence is almost a full stop. There's nothing to be done about it. Knowing who decided and why might provide you more insight going forward, whether for this decision or to understand how to navigate new decisions in the future.

Each stakeholder is a person, as well, meaning a single individual with their own values, constraints, and motivations. While this may seem like obvious information, in practice it matters greatly. If you can interact with a specific stakeholder, you will want to understand them. Knowing how to listen to them and what their concerns and motivations are, will help you deliver what they need at a deeper level. If you understand their constraints, you're in a better position to help them address or work around them.

Adjusting to Each Individual

Because stakeholders are individuals, you will have to learn how to interact with each individual in the way that best suits their personality and needs. Yes, that means you will adjust to them rather than asking them to adjust to you. When you are willing to do this work of adjusting, you earn additional influence to be more easily spent later at need.

Interacting with stakeholders must also be power sensitive and context sensitive. For example, I did a project for a group president in another part of my company, as an internal client high up in the hierarchy. The group president was German and known to be blunt, as he explained, since he had grown up with that communication style. Since I am similarly blunt and straightforward, we interacted very comfortably. The man himself was happy with my work and how I was treating him, even making a point to tell me how much he appreciated me bringing up conflicting opinions.

However, my skip-level boss, the VP of my unit, was in a place to observe my interactions. The VP, who was very concerned with status and appearance, pulled me into his office and chewed me out for being so blunt with the group president. His idea of hierarchy was injured by the interaction even though the group president was happy.

To be clear, I was in the right by treating the group president as he preferred to be treated in a non-group setting. The group president here was my stakeholder. In contrast, in the situation I discussed to begin the chapter, I got in trouble for not being sensitive to context and power. I was focused on my interaction with the participant and not with my stakeholder, the client. I misjudged who my stakeholder was and satisfied the wrong person.

Note that the issue in both cases was *not* whether or not it is appropriate to be blunt or insistent or to disagree in strong terms; it can be correct or incorrect to act in the same way depending on different circumstances. In both cases, however, understanding who my stakeholder was and how I should talk to *him*—and to his clients—was key.

When in doubt, be respectful to everybody, and don't assume you understand the lay of the land when you're first starting out in a new situation. Put on your observer hat, and look for information that tells you more about the ecosystem and its interactions before you make many conclusions. Then be willing to update your understanding as you go.

How to Apply This Chapter

In this exercise, you will identify, categorize, and analyze your stakeholders. Begin with sticky notes and a whiteboard with a four square similar to the one below or create this setup digitally. Here is an example, which I created in an online whiteboarding tool. Before you begin this exercise, consider your own needs. What do you need to understand about your stakeholders? What decisions and actions will it help you with, and how can these tools help you?

(1) Identify. The first step is to identify without sorting. You will identify your stakeholders by taking an inventory of everyone internal to your or your client's organization who has (1) a vested interest in your project and (2) the power, influence, or voice to affect its outcome. Write one name (or title, if you don't know the name) per sticky note, in any order. You can always add more people to your inventory later.

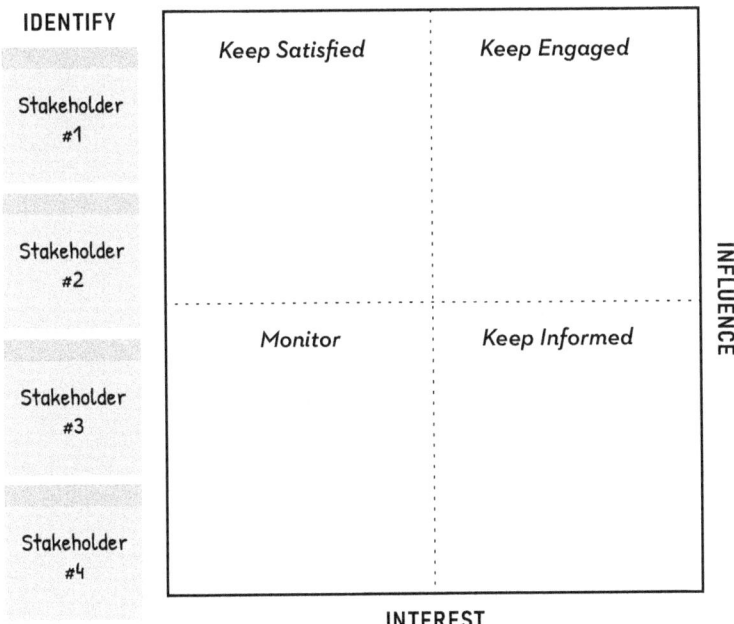

Some questions to ask to help identify stakeholders:

- Who do you communicate with most? What is their role?
- Who do you report or present to?
- Where does your work go from there? Who is seeing the outcomes of your work beyond your immediate supervisors?
- Whose opinion impacts your work the most?
- Who has a vested interest in the outcome of your project? Consider people who may be less obvious, like the example of the manager of the call center for a software company's product.
- Are there any people whom you cannot talk to who will affect your outcomes? If so, who and how?
- Of all the people you've identified, which are the most important to you and the outcome of your project? Who should you approach first?

(2) Categorize. Once you have a working list, categorize each individual stakeholder. I like to sort stakeholders by their interest level (high or low) and their influence (how much say they will have over the project, high or low) in accordance with the four squares pictured above. You may find that different axis labels are better for your situation.

I recommend categorizing by placing each sticky note in one of the four quadrants. If you do not know a piece of the information, place the sticky note in a location designed to cue you to develop that relationship further. This process is iterative, and you may find that stakeholders shift their category over time or that you find other categories more useful in your own work. Hold categories lightly, and be willing to shift as the situation does.

If you are using the categories shown:

- **People with high influence who are interested** and present need to be kept engaged. Make sure they feel heard, even if there are no formal activities for them at a given stage. Include them in updates, and ask for input where appropriate.
- **People with high influence with lower interest** need to be kept satisfied. This is sometimes challenging because they may not be people you can interact directly with and their desired outcomes may be somewhat opaque. Do your best.
- **Engaged people with low influence** must remain informed. In a world with limited time, they cannot be your highest priority, but they can't be ignored because sometimes they grow in influence or can derail established projects. These are your easiest opportunities for allies to the degree you can spare time to court them.
- **Stakeholders who are not engaged and not influential** may still matter over time. Monitor them as possible.

(3) **Analyze**. Once you have done the previous steps, create a system to track important details about each of your most important stakeholders. For an example, I recently chose the following criteria to analyze my four most impactful stakeholders:

- Name
- Role (where they sit in the organization)
- Category (where they sit on the four square above, for reference)
- What they care about

- How well they understand the work
- What they'd like out of the project in exchange for their participation ("engagement objective")
- Degree of contact (how often you talk / how closely you work together)
- Preferred communication method
- How to engage them (working sessions or one-on-one meetings, for example)

These records should operate as your "cheat sheet" to keep you focused and on track with stakeholder communication throughout your project. You'll return to your records again and again to reference what each stakeholder cares about, how they communicate, and how to deliver what they need. You may also want to make notes on how often to reach out and with what purpose.

Two-Minute Summary

Your stakeholders are the people who (1) are internal to your or your client's organization, (2) have a vested interest in the outcome of your work, and (3) have the ability to help or hinder your progress.

- Interacting with stakeholders must be power sensitive and context sensitive to be successful. Take care to address the needs of the correct stakeholder at the correct time.
- Consider the system you are operating within. There will often be important stakeholders you cannot see.
- Stakeholders are individuals, who each have their own values, constraints, and motivations.

- If a decision is made, there is a person who made that decision, and that person can change their mind.
- Update the document you created in the exercise in Chapter One to keep track of your stakeholders and how you should interact with them.

CHAPTER TWO

UNDERSTANDING THE BIG PICTURE

First, develop a good understanding of the overall organization's "big picture" your work and stakeholders are operating within.

I WAS ONCE WORKING WITH A TALENTED, DRIVEN TEAM ON THE user interface for a client project, a small printer operated with a touchscreen. The setup was challenging, given how much needed to be communicated in a space less than two inches wide with working touchscreen functionality. The lead designer was doing excellent technical work. She and her team were following best practices in user experience, working to ensure common user tasks were clear and on the first screen, with less-frequently-used features deeper in the interface.

Unfortunately, the team lost track of one of the company's goals, making it easy to reorder ink from the front screen. (The ink was a major profit center for the company.) In the course of the design work, the front-end designer chose to hide the ink reorder button deeper in the interface so as to better enable navigation through the primary functions. On a communication and end-user experience level, it was a good decision. Users consistently found the new design easier to navigate. However, from the company's perspective, it was not acceptable—hiding the ink reorder button would sharply decrease expected revenue. The stakeholder in charge of the project, Yosef, hinted at the problem during the feedback cycle, but the hints were opaque to the team until the last minute, when he explicitly said no. The team had to scramble to get the changes done by the launch.

As you work on tactical problems, keep in mind there may be bigger strategic goals influencing what the stakeholders are telling you. The big picture may matter more to your outcomes than the strength of the work, so you will need to be cautious. Build as complete a picture as possible of your stakeholder's situation and goals, and apply that picture to the work you're doing.

While the team was told this goal from the beginning, sometimes you will face a big picture you will not be told. It is wise to listen carefully and to apply what knowledge you have. The more you understand about your industry and your stakeholders' world, the better you will be positioned to understand the hints that they give you, and the better you will be able to position your work for success.

Unfortunately, doing everything right on a technical level isn't enough if it does not deliver larger value to the complex system.

Delivering Value

For this chapter, I encourage you to set aside your expertise and perspective for a moment. Before we talk directly to stakeholders, we'll first go on an adventure, considering organizational systems and goals. There we'll find the broader context in which your work will ultimately fit and your stakeholders will operate. Even if you do not use this information immediately, you will eventually need it to interpret what will make your stakeholders happy and to deliver their outcomes long term. When you understand the bigger picture, you are more able to deliver value to your work, to your stakeholders, and to your organization.

You may already know much of what I'll cover here, but a reminder is always helpful.

The Purpose of Organizations

All organizations exist for a reason, though these reasons vary widely. Some organizations exist to make money, while others provide services or work to accomplish a certain mission or end goal. A small subset of mission-driven service businesses may do all three! Your organization's—or your client organization's—specific underlying purpose provides the foundation for its operations.

In order to earn the resources they need to exist, all organizations must provide value to their community or context. In the case of for-profit businesses, the business provides products or services to customers. If enough customers feel there is tangible value in those products or services that they are willing to pay for them, the business will prosper. For nonprofit organizations and government agencies, the case is similar. If the donors, the grant providers, or the budgeters feel that the organization is providing enough value to the community, it will continue to be funded. If the value dries up, the funding may do the same.

What value is your organization providing to the community, your customers, or others? There may be more than one type of value—for example, delivering products to customers and money to shareholders.

Common Organizational Structures
Private (for-profit) business: A private business exists to make money for its owners. Some individual owners may also have

other, secondary goals for the business. For example, a sports team owner may want the team to make the championships, or a local shop may want to provide goods and services that are otherwise not available in the community. A private company can be more subject to individual whims than other types of organizations. This can have a positive or negative result, depending on the knowledge, skill, and vision of the person(s) in charge.

Public (for-profit) business: This type of organization exists as a publicly-traded business owned by its shareholders. The company has a fiduciary responsibility to make its shareholders money, which can take the form of working to increase the stock price or offering dividends to shareholders, among other approaches. The drive towards providing quarter-by-quarter profits for the stock market can sometimes result in short-term thinking in public companies. At the same time, these companies make money by providing goods and services that people are willing to pay for.

Nonprofit organization: A nonprofit exists to carry out a mission or to provide a service for the community. The missions of nonprofits can vary widely, from religious organizations and clubs to community service and public health organizations, among others. Nonprofits must keep their donors and grant providers happy in order to continue their work. In the US, nonprofits have restrictions on activities they can participate in without losing their tax-free status.

Hybrid organization: What I am calling a "hybrid" organization here is a (non-government) organization that is neither a traditional for-profit business nor a nonprofit organization, but contains elements of both. For example, B Corporation (B Corp) and the triple bottom line (TBL) are two frameworks that govern hybrid organizations. The legal and tax implications of a hybrid organization can be complex.

Governmental agency: A government agency exists to carry out a specific, targeted mission on behalf of the government as a whole. Often this mission is to provide public services or to carry out and enforce legislation.

What kind of organization do you work for? What kind of organizations do your stakeholders work for, if different from your own? Are they for-profit, nonprofit, government, or something else? Take a moment and consider your answer.

Finding the Value Proposition

A value proposition is the core of a viable business model. To remain operating, an organization must provide people with *value*—something they want or need enough to pay for it. Organizations that solve a problem a large group of people care about usually become (and remain) successful over time. The value the organization offers the world results in enough money and resources flowing back in to sustain the organization.

Each organization should have a unique *value proposition*. A value proposition should state the value (product, service, or solution) the organization is offering and also highlight:

- **An identifiable set of customers or constituents receiving value**
    - An attractive / realistic market size

- **Why the value provided is significant to customers or constituents**
    - The user experience with and without the solution and benefits received
    - A sustainable business model or price per value created (if it costs more than the organization makes, the organization will quickly go out of business)

- **(Ideally) A way of sustaining a competitive advantage**
    - Why the value offered is unique

Finding Your Organization's Value Proposition

Look around your organization. Who are your customers or constituents? What value do you provide for them?

Customers or constituents: Keep in mind that companies and organizations are not customers; people are. A front-line worker at a manufacturing company will have different problems than an executive at the same company. The same goes for specific groups that a nonprofit or governmental organization serves.

To make it even more complicated, businesses that sell to other businesses have multiple people involved in purchasing. The same goes, to a lesser degree, for government agencies and/or nonprofits. For example, in an enterprise software purchase, you might have:

- The **users** of a technology
- The **decision makers** who will influence whether or not to purchase that technology
- The **buyers** who will ultimately approve the purchase of that technology

In the case of my current company's work contracting and subcontracting for custom government agency software, we may have:

- Citizens who benefit from the service the technology enables
- Other contractors we partner with to deliver a piece of that technology
- The legislators who set overall budgets and priorities for the agency

So you can see that your assessment of "customer" can become layered and complex. Do the best you can, identifying several people or groups if needed.

The problem and the value you provide: What is the problem that your organization is solving? What benefit or value does your specific solution provide to each of your customers? If you work in a very large organization, like GE, Alphabet, or the United Way, focus on the part of the organization you interact with most and the value that part provides.
What is the business model? What benefit does your organization receive in exchange for the value it provides?

Sustaining the solution: In what way is your solution different from that of your competitors? How does your company maintain that difference? Why should your customers go with your solution rather than the alternatives?

Goals and Objectives

Once you can encapsulate the value proposition of the organization in a few sentences, you should turn your attention to goals and objectives. Your organization is *going* somewhere (strategy) and has likely determined what goals and objectives will take it there. In large organizations, specific divisions or business units may have their own distinct strategies and goals. Some organizations and groups don't have a well articulated strategy that guides the choices they make. Nonetheless, choices still need to be made to both accept and turn down opportunities and directions, and even in organizations without explicit strategy, there will be short-term goals and objectives.

Understanding the choices your organization makes will matter greatly to your ability to communicate with your stakeholders. For example, if you are aiming toward one objective and all of your stakeholders are aiming toward a different objective, at best you will struggle to hear each other. At worst your efforts will carry you further and further away from your stakeholders and their objective.

No matter how good the quality of your work, if it is not in the direction of the organization's or stakeholders' goals, it will not be helpful to their cause. You will get more utility out of less effort by heading in the same direction as your stakeholders. Of course, it is possible to help co-create a new path to get to the goal, but you will not receive positive credit for work that leads your organization (or unit) off course.

If the organization (or your division or business unit) has a clear and coherent path that it's traversing, you will need to follow. If, on the other hand, there is no clear strategy, goal, or objective, or if stakeholders are pulling in different directions, that's an issue. The informal strategy that emerges from the morass will be muddy and unhelpful and leave progress against your organization's or division's goals difficult to manage. Fortunately, it's possible to work with your stakeholders to help them focus and prioritize and then to connect your work to this new focused direction. I will share the specifics of how to accomplish this in Chapter Four.

Take a moment and write down any goals and objectives you know of your immediate organization. Note which affect you or your stakeholders directly; these will be particularly important to detail out.

How are Decisions Made?

In addition to the value proposition and immediate objectives of your organization, it's also critical to know how decisions are made within your organization or your client's organization. Decision making power and hierarchy will impact both your stakeholders' and your own career dramatically over time.

Some hierarchical organizations reserve meaningful decision making entirely for executives, who pass decisions down to the rank and file. Other organizations prefer to hold as much decision making as possible at the level of the individual contributor closest to the problems. In these organizations, executives set the goals and make only the highest-level decisions. Of course, a variety of "in-between" and alternate decision-making approaches exist; organizational personalities are as diverse as human ones.

Decision making boils down to one critical question: how much are individuals empowered to make their own decisions? What decisions can they make at what level, and where must they send the decision up the line? If you are an individual, do your specific stakeholders have the agency to make decisions, or are those decisions reserved for people more senior?

Each organization will have specific power dynamics when it comes to decision making. Where are the lines of control, power, and agency? Who influences those decision makers? If you must feed your work up through stakeholders whom you never see, decision making may be more diffuse and complex.

Sometimes you'll be working directly with a stakeholder who is an independent decision maker, whether that's the CEO of a for-profit public company or the director of donor events at a nonprofit. Other times, you must work within a constrained box, within decisions that have already been made and cannot be changed. If you're dealing with an extensive bureaucracy with several steps of decision making, you will need to plan for it. Decisions will take longer and require more time and planning than if you're working with a small startup. Wherever you are on the spectrum of decision making, it's important to understand where you have room to make an impact. What does the organizational landscape look like? Who decides? What can you influence and what must you work within?

Once you know what you can impact, you can avoid the metaphorical "hitting your head against the wall" and instead focus on the areas where your efforts can be most helpful.

Organizations and Industries Change

The structure of organizations will change over time as they grow or shrink, as leadership changes, or as markets shift. The headwinds of the larger world tend to impact industries and organizations in profound ways, leading some to rise to prominence and others to fail.

Technology changes are the classic example. If you were a switchboard operator in the mid-20th century after the invention of automated switching, your job became obsolete. The advent of refrigerators in the home did away with the deliverymen who brought ice door to door. Electronic communications have also drastically impacted the volume of letter mail, affecting my former employer Pitney Bowes.

While some shifts happen over time, enabling organizations to prepare for the shifts, natural disasters can happen suddenly and without warning. These disasters can dramatically shift industries in the short-term with potentially lasting consequences. Hurricane Katrina impacted New Orleans' economy, scattering residents as widely as Atlanta and Tucson, where many stayed. This dramatically affected the workforce for decades afterwards. The COVID-19 pandemic sped the widespread adoption of remote work and the technologies that support virtual engagement and collaboration.

The changing attitudes and demands of everyday people also affect industries. Consumer demand and lobbying has led to a thriving Fair Trade market with companies supporting those policies as a competitive differentiator. Changing attitudes towards LGBTQ+ people means that Pride merchandise is now in big box stores in suburbs and commercials occasionally feature two dads. The growing movement to buy local and organic produce has led to countless farmer's markets in city centers that have driven new businesses, while the movement to adopt plant-based eating has led to the sales of dairy milk dropping dramatically.

Legislation can also be a particularly strong driver of fast change in industries. For example, air bags were not required on cars by law in the US until 1998. The cost of the factory and design changes was immaterial; manufacturers had to comply or lose the ability to sell their products in the US.[3] As another

---

3   https://www.history.com/this-day-in-history/federal-legislation-makes-airbags-mandatory#

example, when Medicare Part D coverage went into effect in 2006, it opened new markets for pharmaceutical companies and created massive opportunities for insurance providers.

Shifts are inevitable, so be aware of what is going on in the larger world. The headwinds that affect your industry *will* change the landscape your organization operates within and the strategies and internal structures it chooses. Organizations are living, dynamic systems, and whether their changes are quick or slow, they will not remain static. Do not expect them to do so.

Bringing Trends Back to Your Situation

Now that you have considered the purpose of your organization and how industries change over time, take a moment and think about what headwinds might affect your organization in the near term future.

- What changing technologies will affect your industry or the industry of your clients?
- Are upcoming legislative changes likely to affect you?
- What social shifts or changing consumer demands may affect your industry or product?
- Have your leaders talked about these changes? If so, how are they planning to respond? If not, how do they seem likely to respond given what you know?
- What strategies are your organization running? Are these strategies likely to be affected by industry and society headwinds?

The answers to these questions will help you understand how the big picture may impact your stakeholders and your own work. For now, let's move from the sweeping headwinds of industries into your specific organization. In the same way that your organization has a purpose within its landscape, your stakeholders have a purpose within theirs.

Where to Get the Big-Picture Information

If any of the information described in this chapter is unclear to you, do not despair. It will take time and effort to build a thorough understanding of your context, and you may never understand everything. Hold your knowledge lightly, and continue to add to it over time.

Don't be afraid to ask your coworkers questions about your organization and the client's organization, and ask for advice. Compare the answers that different coworkers give. Have light conversations with vendors and other people at your level within and without the organization. Once you have built strong relationships with a specific stakeholder (see the next chapter), you may also be able to ask occasional general questions of that person. If they trust you, they will be willing to give you more detailed information about the landscape. (If you're asking whether your relationship with a given person is strong enough to withstand a specific question, it's probably not yet.)

Don't underestimate the value of good search engine work. Read the organization's website, and gather publicly available information. See if the organization is in the news. Read end-of-year reports! For example, the information that leaders choose to include in a for-profit public company's annual report is telling, even though the language is overly optimistic and vague. The leaders are showing you in plain text what they consider important for the company.

If, in the course of your search engine work, you come across publicly available information that impacts your project directly, take note of it. In most cases, you can ask your stakeholders about the impact on the project, and you will look good for having done your homework. Take care though; unless your relationship with your stakeholder is both established and trusted, directly asking about organizational topics beyond the project is unlikely to result in good information and may actually have a negative impact on the relationship.

Note that in all but the most ideal circumstances, you will still have to intuit *some* of the objectives and purposes of the people around you beyond what you are told.

Working with External Organizations

The more time you spend with an organization—assuming you're paying attention—the better understanding you will have of that organization. I worked for Pitney Bowes for fifteen years, for example, and at the end of that stint there wasn't much I didn't know about it. I've also worked with outside organizations for periods varying from three months to multiple years, and the largest driver of organizational knowledge has always been the time I've spent inside. When you work with an outside organization, learn as much as you can using the techniques I just described and the listening work I'll detail in the following chapter. It's important, however, to accept that no amount of work will allow you to fully grasp the strategies of a massive international conglomerate in a three-month stint. Accumulating knowledge will be a slower process from the outside, and while you can be strategic and careful in gathering knowledge, three months is simply not enough time to grasp more than the basics of such a complex system.

I caution you not to kill yourself trying to build a faster-than-possible understanding of either your own or other organizations but also not to get ahead of what you do know. If much of your landscape is sketchy and unknown, approach your decisions softly and with more questions. Leave room to be wrong, and stay in learning mode. Your role is not to teach with an incomplete level of understanding, but rather to listen and to add to your knowledge.

Reading Between the Lines

Judging the strength of the relationship you have with a specific stakeholder is a skill learned through experience. You also learn to read between the lines, to more accurately intuit the context and motivations of your stakeholders to help you interpret their actions over time. Reading between the lines will provide the richest and most accurate (if incomplete) source of information you will get about your stakeholder's big picture.

For example, one of my mid-level researchers was frustrated with one of her stakeholders because she felt he was telling her different things day to day. She pulled me in for help, and since much of their communication was in writing, I was able to offer another perspective. Based on my experience of this particular organization and similar situations with other stakeholders when I was in her role, I was able to see that her stakeholder wasn't changing his bottom-line message at all. Instead, he was being very responsive to internal politics and what would enable decisions to move forward within the organization.

While on the surface it seemed like the stakeholder was saying he wanted X delivered, and then later, Y, there was actually a connection between these things, and they were not mutually exclusive. I suggested my researcher could go to the stakeholder and strategize with him how they could best accomplish his goals. She did exactly that. It turned out that my reading was more or less correct, but there was additional important context. The stakeholder was convinced that the approach we had chosen was the right way, but he was concerned about how to "sell" it internally. So the two brainstormed how to communicate the approach in ways that would resonate with the next level up in the organization. The researcher also added positive suggestions about how to package the deliverables for the best impact.

When I checked in with the researcher and the stakeholder a few weeks later, both were happy with the results of the direction they had chosen. The stakeholder had gotten internal traction and was pleased. The researcher had become more secure in her reading of her stakeholder's motives, and trust had been built on both sides.

As my researcher learned, there are two layers to any given conversation with a stakeholder. There is the first surface level, which in this case was him communicating what he didn't want and asking for changes. The second level of any conversation is the subtext, the layer of implications and references said in passing. The trick is to listen for hints of what the stakeholder actually wants and needs.

Time and experience helps with the process of reading between the lines. You will get better at spotting implications and hints over time—but every organization and context will also require starting from scratch. Approach new situations with a beginner's mind, and trust that you will get faster and more accurate in putting the pieces together as you develop experience throughout your career.

Words and Phrases to Watch For

While you'll develop your own approach to reading between the lines, I have found that the following words, phrases, and circumstances tend to point to something deeper.

The stakeholder says:

- Something new or something you didn't know before, especially when not at the beginning of a project
  - Something incongruous with your understanding of the project or the organization
  - Something that seems to contradict what you think they have said before
  - Something not what you were expecting them to say

- The following indirect or flag words are used:
  - "I'm concerned."
  - "It would be terrible if…"
  - "[Someone else] may be uncomfortable…" or "…may not understand…"
  - "Have you considered…?"

- Communication is highly indirect, especially from a person who normally communicates directly.[4]
  - People will often use very indirect approaches when trying to give you important information that's high stakes, dangerous, political, or just in some way impolite to communicate.

---

4 For many people who are neuroatypical or come from cultures that are very direct, it can be difficult to spot highly indirect communication. In these cases, it becomes particularly important to bring along a colleague to help interpret the subtext of the conversation.

Make sure to apply all your knowledge to every interaction with a stakeholder so that you'll be more likely to spot clues. When you are in a meeting about a tactical "how-to," look for the strategic approach or *why* in the background, and vice versa. Doing so will reveal patterns that may lead to additional insights about the stakeholder's context and situation.

Applying Your Knowledge

Identifying the big-picture priorities and landscape of your stakeholders is of limited use without application; be sure to note and to apply what you learn to your work consistently. Often this means taking a step back and assessing your technical work *before* it's final. Remember the design team from the beginning of the chapter, whose work was excellent from a UX perspective but still failed to highlight the ink reorder? They had to scramble at the last minute to redesign as that decision was unacceptable to the client. You may have to do the same if you do not *apply* your knowledge of the big picture to your specific project.

As you work on tactical problems, keep in mind there may be bigger goals that influence what stakeholders are telling you. Sometimes they will point your work in another direction without making the *why* explicit; if you are being redirected, do not persist in your path, even if that path follows best practices. If the stakeholder is telling you there are other considerations, listen. In the case of this story, the design team had already been told about the strategic initiative; for whatever reason, they proceeded anyway and got themselves in a bad situation. They were able to create another, better design in time, but the scramble would have been avoidable if they had listened.

Sometimes you will not be told how industry trends or agency politics, for example, will impact your work. It is still wise to keep an eye out for that impact and to take heed of your stakeholders' hints as things come up.

Building Resilience

When you take the time to understand the big picture of your organization, your client's organization, and your stakeholder's world, you increase your impact. Paying attention to the big picture means that you will be more effective and more resilient at your job and see your work go further.

Resilience is the key. The big picture is a changing, evolving thing; part of success in any technical role is to be able to ride the waves of change and to continue to bring our work to bear in a positive direction. While it would be nice if we could learn our set of skills to a high level and simply do our jobs over and over without change, that is not the world we live in. All industries and all organizations change over time, and we must change with them. Don't allow yourself to grow complacent; remain adaptable and resilient so that you can see what direction the wind is blowing and adjust the direction of your sails to match. That is the only way to continue to have the impact you want to have over the long term.

How to Apply This Chapter

Answer the following questions for your organization and/or each client's organization. (You may need to do search engine work or ask colleagues to answer some of the questions.) If you don't know an answer for certain, even after legwork, make an educated guess and mark your guess with a question mark. If you are new to an organization, your answers may be mostly question marks. This is fine, so long as you continue to learn and flesh out more certain answers over time.

For each organization you're working with:

- What type of organization is it?
    - For example, is it for-profit, nonprofit, or government?
- What industry is the organization operating within?
- Is that industry getting bigger or smaller?
- What additional changes or headwinds are impacting that industry or are likely to do so in the future?
- What industry or group does the organization serve?
- How are decisions made in the organization? If by a small number of people, list them by name or title.
- If you know any, what forces are influencing your stakeholders in specific?
- What are the organization's immediate goals and objectives?

Two-Minute Summary

You are a small part of a big picture. Understanding even *some* of the big picture of your stakeholders' organization(s) and industr(ies) allows you to be more effective and more resilient.

- Organizations provide value in exchange for resources.
- Different business models operate in different ways. For-profit, nonprofit, and government organizations, for example, are rewarded for different things.
- Industries and organizations change over time.
- The goals of the organization will help to drive the goals of your stakeholder(s).
- Gather big-picture information from what stakeholders say in passing, light conversations with your coworkers and vendors, and diligent search engine work over time.

CHAPTER THREE

LISTENING TO YOUR STAKEHOLDERS

To get what you want from your stakeholders, you need to listen to them and truly understand their perspective. In this chapter, you'll learn how to do that in practice.

ONE OF MY FRIENDS IS A DIRECTOR FOR A LARGE COMPANY THAT outsources the ongoing maintenance and development of their website to an external vendor. She is responsible for overseeing the vendor's ongoing work. We'll call the lead on the vendor side Arnold and my friend, his stakeholder, Isabella.

Every week or two, Isabella has a meeting with Arnold, which is supposed to ensure that his company is delivering their priorities in a reasonable timeline. Instead, Arnold is coming to these meetings with a list of things *he* wants to tell Isabella—not topics to ask her input on, not questions he has for her, but a long list of facts and situations he wants her to know. Now Isabella is a profoundly patient person, which might be to her detriment, because it took four months for her to get fed up.

"I can't get a word in edgewise," she told me. "He doesn't listen to what I'm saying when I do fight my way into talking. And he changes the subject as fast as I bring something up. It's maddening. I don't know yet if I have the power to get him replaced on the project, but I'm going to try."

A year later, Isabella was thrilled to say her company had switched vendors. Arnold's company had failed to make important changes because he had failed to listen to Isabella's communications in meetings. Her bosses had already been on the fence about the provider, and based on her experience and the experience of several others, the company had decided the cost of the switch was worthwhile.

Arnold missed the most fundamental part of talking to stakeholders—that the skill is ninety percent about *listening*.

Stakeholder Relationships Are About Listening

Like Arnold, many technical specialists come into meetings with a list of things they want stakeholders to understand. I find this attitude is nearly always a mistake. *Why* do you need your stakeholder to understand X, Y, or Z? Is that for your benefit or their benefit? If the list exists to make your work better or easier, the list is leading you astray. You are there to support the stakeholder and their priorities—act accordingly.

The correct approach to a stakeholder meeting is to flip the script. What does the stakeholder need to know for their benefit? What does the stakeholder need from this meeting to support their values and priorities? How can you help them get where they need to go? If you're making the meeting about you, the stakeholder won't care, whereas if you're making it about their needs, they will pay close attention.

If you aren't listening to your stakeholder, you will inevitably fail to put what you're saying into terms that they can relate to and buy into. Getting understanding *from* them requires listening *to* them. It also requires considering their point of view and working towards active collaboration. Otherwise, they will disengage.

Make Them Feel Heard

Some stakeholders won't mind a small amount of talking past each other if the work is done, but most will find the lack of connection frustrating and counterproductive. When they do not get a chance to say what they want to say, stakeholders will not respond well, and the relationship will suffer.

Feeling heard is a basic human need in every arena. No one wants to go on a second date with someone who spends the entirety of the first date talking about himself. The same is true in business. If you want people to like you, to trust you, and to work with you collaboratively, help them feel heard. Otherwise, you risk irritating your stakeholder as much as Arnold irritated Isabella.

In addition, the critical information you need to make your project a success *comes directly from listening*. If you do not listen to your stakeholders, it shows you do not trust their knowledge and do not want their input. If you do not ask about your stakeholders' wants and needs in the project and do not listen, how can you know how to succeed? A project that delivers technical expertise but none of the stakeholders' goals is a beautiful failure.

Listening is the unsung secret of the workplace. It builds the vocabulary, the relationship, and the context you will need to communicate with your stakeholders long term and to deliver the impact you want.

Relationships Protect You

Not to overemphasize the point, but listening is highly beneficial *for you*. Listening opens doors for you that technical skills alone will not. It buys you trust, forbearance, and opportunities to correct mistakes. When people like you and trust you, they open up to you over time. You will have more honest conversations and be able to ask the kinds of big-picture questions we highlighted in the last chapter. If you listen, stakeholders may eventually be willing to discuss specific internal dynamics of their organization when you ask them. Your ability to understand the landscape and anticipate changes coming in your project will naturally increase, as will your impact.

The relationship itself will also protect you. We all feel warmer feelings towards the people who listen to us than the people who talk at us. People you have a good relationship with, who like you and trust you, will put you forward and say good things about you. They will stick up for you when you are not in the room. They will send more opportunities your way—including future jobs and projects—and give you the benefit of the doubt. They will become your ally and not your enemy. Relationships are inherently valuable.

Having allies with influence is also immensely helpful in hard times. When a downturn arrives and people are chosen for layoffs, the people without excellent work get cut first. Then the harder cuts happen. When decision makers have to choose between two people with excellent work, they'll choose to keep the one they like and trust.

Listen to Problem Solve

The relationships you build when you *listen* and when you're known for listening will provide a career advantage for you. Not only can you position your work for better impact, you'll be able to get ahead of problems—sometimes even problems in other teams—in time to solve them effectively. Failing to listen, on the other hand, leads to compounding issues.

I'll give you an example. In a former company, one of my direct reports came to me for advice in dealing with a particularly challenging stakeholder we'll call Betty. I listened to my team member and let her vent at length before it became obvious that I didn't have enough information to understand the situation. All I could tell was that the team had not gone to Betty to try to hear her perspective. I suspected a miscommunication.

I did not know Betty, but I had worked on this project before my promotion, and so I had a good relationship with the former client partner in charge, whom we'll call Tyrone. He was still at the client company but had been moved to a senior role. I reached out to him, and Tyrone was thrilled to hear from me. We talked for an hour, and Tyrone opened up about Betty, who was challenging from his side as well. He gave advice on how I might be able to meet with her, telling me that my team hadn't tried to do so. He also told me point-blank that our team needed to make changes as the work at this point wasn't going well. I thanked Tyrone and met with Betty before going back to the team.

The team was able to address Betty's priorities and deliver her and Tyrone's overarching goal for the project on time with a minimum of communication issues. I am proud of the team and of my direct report; I have seen similar situations go badly when teams double down on their frustrations. If you assume that the stakeholder is at fault and cut yourself off from them when difficulties arise, you won't have the opportunity to hear their feedback, and the project will eventually blow up or end in a whimper. What you do not know, you cannot fix.

My relationship with Tyrone provided a useful shortcut to the information we needed and that should also not be discounted. When you build relationships of trust, stakeholders want you to succeed. They help you, they give you feedback you can use to improve, and they help you strategize a good path forward.

Listening provides the key to these relationships and to the improvement opportunities they bring.

When you face a difficult stakeholder, find a colleague to lay out the problems to. Articulate everything that's wrong, vent, and express your frustration. Then step away from it for long enough to calm down. When you come back, consider what you can do differently. Often, beginning with *listening* will provide a resolution, even if that resolution comes by way of difficult changes. (If you're facing a stakeholder who doesn't respond to listening and basic relationship building, see chapter 7 for additional techniques to employ.)

Deliver on Their Terms

This is not a book about collaboration and meeting people in the middle, though those are useful skills to use with coworkers. Instead, this is a book about delivering outcomes and value for your stakeholders, who are in a position to positively impact your work and career. For better or worse, the power sits with the stakeholder. That fact creates opportunities, but it also drives realities that may not be pleasant.

Think of it in terms of defensive driving. The problem on the road may not be you—your driving may be fine—but to avoid an accident, you must take responsibility for the situation anyway. You must figure out how to fix the problem from your end. The power disparity of the relationship with the stakeholder drives a similar dynamic. You may not be given a 50-50 situation; to make the relationship work, you might have to give 90 percent of the effort. That's not fair, but it is the reality. In most cases, you can still be successful.

Listening is always the first step. Once you understand your stakeholder's goals, you can frame your work in terms they will understand. You can deliver more useful value to them and earn their trust as a reliable and competent partner. Over time, you build a relationship that earns you the right to advise them at a different level; they give you more leeway and rely more often on your guidance. They trust you to deliver the best options and to tell them the truth. That trust gives you more authority and influence, which in turn enables your work to have more impact.

The road to the impact you want starts with understanding what matters to your stakeholder. Listen, understand, and then help.

Reframing Your Work to Matter to Your Stakeholder

A few years ago, I oversaw several teams of researchers and designers, one of which was led by designer Naomi. The software project was mission critical for the client and the stakeholder Charles saw research as a box to check and design as simply visual. He was very concerned that Naomi's team's work was slowing down the mission-critical project and snapped at her when she tried to explain the importance of user experience. He was also very reactive; priorities for the project would constantly shift, making it hard for all of the teams to keep up, but the stress was greatest on Naomi's team.

Fortunately, after the third blow-up, Naomi came to me, and we compared notes. I was able to point to the likely problem: reactivity is nearly always driven by fear and risk aversion. Naomi and I were able to go to Charles and have a careful conversation to understand his perspective on the risks that most worried him. I and the rest of the teams adjusted our approach, and Naomi and her team were then able to switch the language of their conversations with Charles from user experience to the UX impact on his mission. We earned extra trust as a result, and Naomi and her team used this additional trust to demonstrate the value of their work.

In the end, because the work was framed around something Charles cared about, he paid more attention and was more patient, and the teams could directly address the real issues that made the project successful. When he heard something that concerned him in a presentation by Naomi's team, he sent her a quick message on Slack with questions instead of insisting on immediate changes. They were able to dialogue, him asking questions and her reassuring him, which was a vast change from their past interactions. When I checked in a few weeks later, both were happy with the progress they had made in their working relationship.

You May Change Your Perspective

By far the most important reason to listen to your stakeholder is that you need the information they will give you if you are going to be successful. Regardless of how senior or junior your stakeholder is or what set of skills they bring to the table, they will have access to information that you do not by virtue of their position. They will have built a specific perspective, and you may find that if you listen it changes your mind.

All of us have strengths and weaknesses at work, and all of us can operate from mistaken assumptions. Being open to additional information and perspectives provides valuable double-checks that benefit everyone.

In the end, you are there to deliver what the stakeholder wants and needs out of the project, and listening makes that process infinitely easier.

An Example of a Changed Perspective

My friend Ralph is a lawyer, who was recently working on a multiparty discrimination case in emergency proceedings where his team was focused on legal strategy. As he described it, the client was constantly blocking him, slowing down the progress of the case. When he in frustration sat her down to ask why, he discovered she was focused on a different concern. She was worried the names of those involved in her organization would become public and that her colleagues would be subjected to threats or violence. She showed Ralph truly frightening threats which the organization had already received and said that some members were scared to sign declarations. Ralph was floored. He went to the team with a profoundly changed perspective.

Two weeks later, he and his team had figured out how to prioritize the privacy and safety of the organization's members while still fighting the legal battles effectively. In the process, they learned more about the real people who had been part of the decisions being contested. Ralph laughed, "It's ironic. I found the story I used in the closing argument that way, and it gave us extra ammunition in court."

As a different colleague recently told me, "Sitting with stakeholders *always* gives me a better idea of what they want for an outcome. It also gives me opportunities to guide them in what is possible within the time frame, budget, or capacity of the team." And sometimes, like with Ralph's case, listening changes everything.

The Mechanics of Listening Take Effort

How then should you listen? In the research field, we explicitly teach the mechanics of listening, and I have found the same approach to be helpful in meetings with stakeholders. I recommend doing a deeper study of the skill, but in the meantime, here are some useful principles and advanced listening skills to allow your conversations to be more productive and to get more information out of your stakeholders than you might otherwise be able to.

- Keep the power relationship in the stakeholders' favor.
- Let them take the lead.
- Don't barrage them with questions.
- Let them provide information they think is important.
- Make them feel like they're experts—they are.
- Be respectful.
- Don't disrupt the environment – you are a guest and stranger.
- Be interested in what they have to say.
- Concentrate on the answer, not your next question.
- Make eye contact.
- Be comfortable with silence.
- Allow pauses in the conversation for them to think or add details.
- Don't interrupt.
- Don't jump in as soon as they take a second to breathe.
- Use positive reinforcement to show you're listening: nodding, uh-huh, etc.
- Seem interested, even if you're not!
- Be aware of their body language.
- Be aware of your body language; avoid slouching, looking around the room, etc.

You'll notice from the list that advanced listening means attending to the conversation and letting the other person lead.

It also requires the discipline of leaving some time after they stop talking before you respond. This practice ensures they're done talking and have added whatever additional details they were considering. If instead you rush to talk, you risk your stakeholder feeling as Isabella did with Arnold in the story that starts the chapter—talked over and dismissed.

Pausing before responding is also a good practice in a conversation because it ensures you're not rushing to say the next thing. It allows you to fully process what has been said before you respond. Use that gap, rather than the time your stakeholders are talking, to plan what you will say. In doing so you'll not only *demonstrate* that you are listening, but you'll actually hear and retain more of what is being said.

Now that you have a solid grasp of listening, let's apply that skill to the more general work of relationship building.

Intentional Relationship Building

Relationships will not form without intentional effort that begins with, but is not limited to, the work of listening. Fortunately there are specific steps that you can take to develop relationships intentionally, beginning with asking questions. When you are introduced to a new stakeholder, ask what success will look like to them in the project and pay attention to their answers. Read between the lines to intuit what their answers mean about their priorities and values and continue to adjust your understanding as you go. (We'll return to this theme later in the chapter.)

Also, do not neglect the daily opportunities to build a human connection through small talk. When you're meeting for the first time, especially in a group, initiate introductions or an icebreaker. Find opportunities for low-stakes personal details to be discussed and lean into small talk. Technical people often skip this step, but the "pleasant noise" of the personal details add up to relationships and trust over time.

If you are positioned to do so, ask for a one-on-one meeting with your stakeholder early in your relationship and periodically thereafter. Often people won't accept a business meeting simply to talk, so it's best to frame that meeting as wanting to better understand some specific aspect of the project. Choose some piece of the project that you would benefit from additional information on, and set up the meeting.

Early in the relationship, you should aim for 90 percent of your time spent listening to your stakeholder, rather than meeting them halfway. Over time they'll begin to reciprocate until a more established relationship looks like a 50-50 split. Even there, though, if you are going to err on one side or the other, listen more than you speak. (This dynamic does *not* mean you have to agree with everything they say, but merely that you are making more of the effort to connect and follow up.)

In this initial conversation and in the others after it, don't *just* talk about business. Show interest in your stakeholder as a person. Ask about their kids, their dog, and their favorite vacation spot, especially at the beginning of meetings. Don't ask about their darkest secrets or spend the entire meeting on personal details, but get to know them. Listen to who they are beyond the transactional level of work.

Questions to Ask

Low-stakes questions to ask when you first meet someone include:

- Where do you live? (Especially natural in our current era of Zoom-driven meetings.)

- What's the weather like right now where you are?[5]
- Do you have any hobbies?
- What's your favorite food?
- Do you have a favorite sports team?
- Have you seen any good movies (or plays) recently?

You can generally ask any "softball" chatty question about a topic people will discuss readily with strangers. (Try to steer clear of politics and religion; in some areas of the country that boycott should extend to sports as well.)

Personal but "not too personal" questions to get to know established stakeholders include:

- Do you have kids?
- You mentioned a dog. What kind of dog is it?
- What are you doing this weekend?
- What did you do over the weekend?
- Do you like desserts? Coffee?
- What are your favorite vacation spots?

Careful Reciprocity

Small talk is most effective when it feels reciprocal. Aim to listen more than you speak and not to take over the conversation, but volunteer similar information: if you ask about their dog, bring up your own dog. People like and trust people they have things in common with, so look for and talk about these points of commonality. You may not create a lifelong friendship (though you might!), but you will make a connection. Small talk helps smooth relationships and makes them feel less transactional.

---

5   Unless either of you works for The Weather Channel, is a broadcaster working in the weather, or works for a meteorological organization. In which case, this question is not small talk–it's work!

Small talk should usually take no more than five to ten minutes at the beginning of a meeting or while waiting for others to arrive. Longer meetings can support a little more discussion than shorter ones, though you will want to follow the cues of your stakeholder when it comes time to transition to work topics.

Adjust to Your Stakeholder's Style

Since I have recommended asking about peoples' pets, children, and hobbies, I should also mention that not everyone loves small talk of this nature. Some people can find small talk annoying. They often value efficiency and straightforward communication instead.

Pay attention to the small cues you get from your stakeholder. How do the people they work with treat them? What do they appreciate? Do they value detailed and frequent communication? Do they value terseness and being left alone except when they are needed? Do they want to see the evidence of your work along the way or would they prefer to just see the final product? When you understand how your stakeholder works, you can adjust your working style to their preferences wherever possible and so ensure a better experience for both of you.

For example, in a recent project, the client replaced their primary stakeholder for user experience. Suddenly, we were running into major communication challenges, which took time to tease out. The previous stakeholder had thrived on knowing every small change that happened, so all six designers were used to going to the stakeholder for every small detail. The new stakeholder, on the other hand, had been assigned a large stable of projects, and the constant barrage of small details became a problem for her.

Finally, the new stakeholder took our manager aside and said plainly, "I can't have all this stuff coming at me. Come to me when you need big-picture approval for something final, not with all this stuff the managers should be handling." She promised to keep office hours, but she wanted to be hands-off with the details, in direct opposition to her predecessor.

What's surprising is how difficult the team found the adjustment. For months, they worried because she felt so distant. She had other responsibilities; whereas they spent 100 percent of their time on the project, she could only spend 25 percent of hers. I counseled one designer that she needed to be more considerate. Stakeholders may have different values simply because they have different demands on their time. In fact, that dynamic is more common than not: the more senior someone becomes, the more differing responsibilities they will have and the more context switching they must do on a regular basis. Be patient, and be willing to do the work to bridge the gap.

Relationships Require Maintenance

Just like any other relationship, a solid working relationship with your stakeholder will take an ongoing investment of time. In many cases, that time will naturally occur as part of a work project, as long as you continue to invest in small talk. In others, you will need to find opportunities to "catch up" if it's been some time since you've been in touch—try to do this once a month or at least once a quarter if monthly is too often for your stakeholder.

Look for places to ask for advice, to reconnect, or to ask for feedback to keep the conversation going. If you're looking for an opportunity to connect with a challenging stakeholder you don't know well, reach out to one you *do* know well on the same program, and ask for their opinion, even if it's been a year or two since you've talked. Stakeholders you've built relationships with in the past will nearly always be happy to hear from you. Those relationships, and your relationships with colleagues and former colleagues, provide valuable resources as you grow in your career.

Now that I've discussed how to build more human relationships and how often to talk and to listen, let's turn to the question of *what* we're listening for.

Understand What Drives Your Stakeholder

The goal of listening, of small talk, and of asking good professional questions is the same: building an understanding of what drives your stakeholder. Ask personal questions gently to build the relationship, and ask professional ones to build understanding. What do they care about as a person in their life? Why are they a stakeholder for your project? What does success look like in their terms? Listen carefully to the passing comments that tend to illuminate someone's values and priorities.

What piece of the project most directly impacts their goals? They may be judged on your work as part of *many* objectives or be overwhelmed with competing priorities. Take the time to understand their world and how your work can support them so that you can target your work to be maximally successful.

Understanding Stakeholder Objectives

Regardless of *what* those objectives are, each stakeholder will be driving towards a specific set of them. Some may be goals the organization has assigned to them. Others may be self-directed but no less important. Each objective will also be attached to a deeper *why* or multiple *whys*. They may also add to or take away from the *whys* of other stakeholders.

The most powerful question to ask a stakeholder is, "What does success look like for you, and why?" Not only will you receive information about the objectives you will be directly responsible to work towards, you will also get contextual knowledge about the landscape and what is important in their world. Pay attention when people are talking to each other in meetings, particularly when the meeting involves an external organization. Often people will reference important information in passing, and you'll be able to reconstruct it based on context.

On one of our projects last year, a very good researcher was presenting her work to the client stakeholder. The researcher was understandably focused on giving a good presentation, but the stakeholder was communicating indirectly. Fortunately, I had decided to sit in on the meeting; I was able to pick up the small details that the researcher didn't catch because of her focus on her work. The point is not to put a spotlight on my role, but rather to highlight the importance of sending two people. The presenter will not be able to listen for the level of implications you will need. Having two people allows you to process and to compare notes for an even deeper understanding.

Watch Out for Emotional Investment

Many stakeholders will interact with your project because they were assigned to it. Others may voluntarily choose to get involved, often because they care about the outcome of the project even if it is not assigned to them. A stakeholder who cares intensely about the outcome often brings additional challenges: the emotional investment often means they have strong opinions and care about getting their way. They may be less open to input from others, even if that input is supported by data. People who deeply care about a cause or situation may need extra help defining positive outcomes. They may be less patient and more anxious or faster to dictate priorities; you will need to *listen* to determine how they are interacting with the project you are working on and what additional support, if any, they need to feel that the work has been successful.

Listening to this stakeholder is more involved than the one who is there to achieve a straightforward goal; if you are involved with one or more of these stakeholders, it is especially important to understand where they sit in the organizational hierarchy and to build allies with those who can influence them when needed.

Conversations Shift over Time

Listening to your stakeholder gives you critical information you need to make your project successful. Ask questions to gather that information, but be cautious about asking direct and probing questions of stakeholders new to you. In the beginning, your questions will need to remain largely focused on the specific project. As you develop rapport with your stakeholder, you will slowly earn their trust, and they may drop more details into the conversation—sometimes subtly, sometimes directly. These details may indicate their specific worries or even point you toward organizational politics you may not have been aware of. These details can be immeasurably helpful to know as you target your work to help them solve problems. (I'll show you how to do that specifically in Chapter Four.)

Try to match the level of your conversation to the level of the relationship and trust you have built, and let your stakeholder take the lead on opening up more. If you question whether you have the relationship standing to ask something specific, it's likely you don't; when in doubt, stay more shallow and work-focused until more trust is earned.

Questions to Ask at the Beginning of a Project

As your next project begins, ask your stakeholder or stakeholders the following questions. You may also want to add your own.

- What does success look like to you?
- What outcomes would you like?
- Who else has an interest in this that I may not know about?
- What would you consider to be a failure?
- How would you prefer I communicate with you?

Of course much of the critical information you will need will not come up from questions; you'll need to listen carefully and read between the lines as discussed earlier in the chapter. I'll discuss what to listen for and then come back to advice on how to observe to gain this information if you cannot ask for it directly.

What to Listen For

Building relationships with stakeholders happens over time, as does building an understanding of what they want and need. You will not be able to gather all of the following information all at once. In some cases, you will be operating from a partial understanding or assumptions and adding to your knowledge from things said in passing. Still, I recommend having a mental or physical record[6] of the following information for each stakeholder.

---

6   If you create records in writing about your stakeholders, be certain to store that information securely in a way that's unlikely to be anything but private to you. Even then, be certain to describe information in neutral or positive terms whenever possible; anything that exists in writing has the possibility of being read, and you will not want a negative opinion of a stakeholder getting back to him or her.

- **Their *goals*:** Objectives that they're working towards and being held accountable for, which may or may not be connected to your project.
- **Their *values*:** The intangible things they care about, which may include ideal behavior and ethical standards as well as their personal definition of excellence.
- **Their *work style:*** What communication do they appreciate and at what time? Do they value terseness or thoroughness?
- **Other responsibilities:** Your stakeholder will be responsible for things other than your project. How do those impact them and you?
- **Their *interest* in the project:** Why are they a stakeholder on your project? What about this work matters to them? What are they trying to get out of it?
- **Other parties:** Who else in your stakeholder's world may be interested in the project? Are there any you may not see?

As I get to know a stakeholder and their situation, I tend to remember the important details and to update them as I go. I also try to remember pets' names and people's children; I studied anthropology and I have an affinity for details of this nature. So I'm not the best person to give you detailed advice on how to record this information in writing. That being said, I've heard of people keeping notes in their contact book, in CRMs, in the notes app in their phone, or in the files for the project. However you choose to record the information, do so.

Ask for More Information

You will not always be able to ask direct questions of your stakeholder, particularly if the relationship is new or highly transactional. The skill of reading between the lines (discussed in the last chapter) is also particularly useful in this context. However, don't neglect the art of the question. Even in a transactional relationship, you can ask, "Why do you say that? Could you explain more?" You can ask for clarification on what they meant by a word or a phrase. People like talking about themselves and their expertise. They are often happy to give information, to help you understand something, or to help the work be done right. Yes, this tactic requires the intellectual humility to admit that you do not know something, which can feel scary to many people. It's still far better to do that voluntarily, rather than your lack of understanding becoming obvious when you get something important wrong.

When you ask a stakeholder for more information, it also benefits the relationship. Most people are happy to talk more about the thing they are passionate about. They feel heard and their opinion valued. When you ask them for details, you're deferring to their knowledge and respecting their position as the stakeholder. That deference will lead to a better relationship and more help from your stakeholder. As we've learned in the research field, humility can open doors and keep them open in ways arrogance cannot.

I'll repeat again that deferring to your stakeholder in no way means reflexively agreeing with them in every detail. It means, instead, that you are respecting their position and earning more trust for your expertise. In some cases, adjusting to your stakeholder will mean being *more* forthright and decisive to suit their working style rather than your own.

How to Deal with Multiple Competing Stakeholders

Up to this point, we've assumed you're dealing with one or two important stakeholders whose wants and needs are not clashing with each other. The real world is often much messier with one person pushing the project in a direction fundamentally incompatible with another. Resolving these conflicts can be tricky.

For example, at one point in my career I was dealing with a pair of stakeholders on a critical project. One, who I will call Nisha, was challenging to work with, and I had an easier rapport with the other, Scott. In one-on-ones, Scott would tell me the work was great, and then go into a meeting with Nisha who didn't like it. Scott would get on board with Nisha, and I would have to redo work based on the new priorities. To solve this problem, I went back to my records and reviewed what was important to each of them and how each preferred to be interacted with. Then I got Scott and Nisha in a room with the official decision maker (who had been hands off to that point) to iron out priorities and how to approach the work moving forward. Fortunately, once everyone felt heard, there was a clear path to address everyone's concerns.

Tracking stakeholders with the tools introduced in the Chapter One exercise can be immensely helpful to clarify how everyone responds best. If Nisha's needs were heard, then asking her for advice on how to handle a change might smooth the situation. If Scott's bottom line was to incorporate XYZ priority, I could ensure that priority was featured in the final work even if other changes were made by another stakeholder.

When you face a group of stakeholders, get clear on who the actual decision maker is. Politely take everyone's input, fully understand that input, and then defer to the decision maker.

That's the easy path. If there are two decision makers, clarify where and when each makes decisions within their purview. Sometimes, though, it's not clear who the decision maker is, or there are several with equal power who cannot all be equally satisfied. In that case, it becomes critical to get everyone in the same room.

One of the best ways to resolve a stakeholder input clash is to "play dumb." Tell the person who's offering direction you're confused. "You're saying this, but I think John said that. Can we all talk together to make sure I understand?" Then set up a working session to resolve the issue jointly with the stakeholders involved, rather than trying to please everyone individually or getting caught in between.

Listening Is the Key

Don't be like Arnold, who began the chapter by talking more than he listened and making himself a pest as a result. Showing up with a list of things for the stakeholders to understand means you're putting your own thoughts and ideas ahead of your stakeholders'. You're not giving them room to tell you what matters to them in the project and overall. At best, you'll have a strained, transactional relationship. At worst, you'll miss critical information, and the project will blow up on you.

How to Apply This Chapter

Create or expand your stakeholder records if you have not done so already, filling in whatever information you already have.

Then make a plan for *how* and *when* you will reach out to connect with your stakeholders and any other parties you have time to approach. How often will you talk to them? What questions will you ask them? What information should you listen for? Then block out time or set reminders for yourself to follow up with each specific person with their preferred method. If you have another reason (or excuse) to contact them in the meantime, you can ignore the reminder, but you will want to be sure to follow up regularly.

Whatever else you ask, be sure that you discover what each stakeholder considers success and what objectives must be met.

Two-Minute Summary

Listen to your stakeholders to understand their perspective and to be able to address them using their language.

- Relationships with stakeholders are inherently worthwhile to build. Feeling heard is a basic human need, so listening builds relationships.
- You need the information you will get from listening.
- Set up times to meet with your stakeholders, and spend the time on small talk to get to know them as people, even during work meetings.
- Ask questions to understand what drives your stakeholders.
- Identify and adjust to their working style, and figure out what they need from you.
- If you have a group of stakeholders who don't agree, get them to talk to each other.
- Flesh out your stakeholder records to keep track of what you learn from each stakeholder.

CHAPTER FOUR

HELPING WITH YOUR STAKEHOLDERS' PROBLEMS

Once you understand your stakeholders' goals, how do you help them get there? In this chapter, you'll learn techniques for framing the specific problem space, guiding the conversation, and collaborating and prioritizing solutions for the most impact.

IN MY FIELD, WE ARE WARY OF CLIENTS WHO WANT A SOFTWARE "platform" because they often want that platform to be all things to all people and to solve their problems immediately. Unfortunately, that's unrealistic and not how software or humans work. The lack of focus tends to hurt outcomes; without a focused value proposition, a "platform" becomes a tangle of ideas and may not come to fruition at all.

Many years ago, I was on a team implementing a platform to enable electronic bills receipt and payments. That functionality is table stakes these days, but in that era it was new. My boss on the project was interfacing with the stakeholders and did not like telling anyone no. This turned out to be a slow-moving disaster.

We started the project in the right way, looking at the trends in the industry and where the technology was going. We looked at our company's strengths and what users wanted and needed. Then we came into ideation sessions to determine what the software would actually be like. My boss at the time didn't want to take up the time of executives and told them they did not need to be part of the data gathering and analysis that led up to the ideation sessions. So not all of the stakeholders were on board with the same priorities. We ended up with three broad areas that each could have taken up a whole team for more than a year.

Then the stakeholders who had not been engaged started showing up with "small requests" that changed the requirements of the system, asking for marketing opportunities and ways to data mine. Suddenly we were spread so thin we couldn't gather enough data to make a roadmap. Nothing was ever fully completed. We kept moving between tasks for six months, working on whatever piece felt most urgent until the stakeholders finally pulled the plug. It was a nightmare.

Just like with our platform project, an unclear problem or lack of prioritization will set you and your work up for failure. If you try to be all things to all people, you will deliver nothing to no one. Success means focusing your work, framing the problem space, and *prioritizing* for the most impact.

Good Work Isn't Enough

Every one of the people working on that project was a competent technician in their chosen field. No one slacked off or failed to show up every day willing to work hard. In the absence of other things, though, our skills and our diligence alone weren't enough. We also felt incredibly frustrated, ping-ponging from initiative to initiative without being able to finish any one.

I can't tell you how many projects I have seen where the stakeholder asks for constant small changes and teams complete ticket after ticket with small but urgent tasks. Then, at the end of the allotted period, the stakeholder is angry because they haven't gotten any of the outcomes they wanted. Work gets done, and teams are constantly busy, but there isn't a measurable outcome. This, too, is a failure state, and one that this chapter is designed to help you avoid. I'll walk you through how to help your stakeholder define their problem and ideal outcome and define their priorities so that your work can deliver meaningful outcomes. That is how you earn impact and influence long term. (It is also, incidentally, how you do your best technical work, focused on the right things for prolonged periods.)

Good work alone isn't enough. It has to be the right work, to solve the right problem, in the right context, to deliver the right outcomes. And that right work has to begin with the willingness to choose to do some work deliberately in a focused way.

Fortunately, there's a lot that you can do to facilitate this focus.

Putting a Stake in the Ground

Stakeholders are human too, and humans tend to want to put off difficult decisions. Choosing between several things you want is by definition a difficult decision, particularly in the context of work, where peoples' livelihoods and careers can be impacted. Unfortunately, by choosing *not* to choose, they and you set your project up for the same kind of failure we experienced in our platform project.

One of your most important roles in talking with stakeholders is to act as a trusted advisor and help them make hard decisions. That means creating structure and setting boundaries at times. My boss in the story that begins the chapter did us no favors; by not wanting to say no, she made our lives and our stakeholders' lives much more difficult.

Often stakeholders need assistance in focusing and in deciding for themselves what is most important. Busy people often have a thousand things screaming at them for attention with a lot of pressure to solve all of them immediately. I recommend being sensitive to the demands they are facing, but it is your role to help them decide. Of the many things they'd like to do, what is most important? What exactly is the problem that you are here to solve, and what would a good solution look like?

Only once you've framed the problem, can you help to determine the right path to the solution. Only then can you situate your work for the most impact to create the outcomes that matter.

I've worked with stakeholders who put a great deal of pressure on small details, and I've worked with stakeholders who have been stubbornly hands-off. I have a lot of sympathy for the difficulty of pushing back against forceful stakeholders who seem to hold all of the cards. Yet, by deferring to excess, you end up failing your stakeholders by other means.

Put a stake in the ground; insist on *deciding* something. Certainly you and your stakeholders can make a decision lightly and get additional information to possibly find out you're wrong. You can iterate and make a different decision. But to move forward you must guide your stakeholders to decide with conviction. Hold your beliefs lightly, and be open to input and change, but have the moral courage to insist on making a working decision in the meantime.

Get Your Stakeholders Involved

Often success means fighting the tendency of stakeholders to be hands-off. We often feel like we have to execute on tasks we've been assigned and bring results back fully formed. This is a dangerous dynamic. Whenever possible, work to get your stakeholders more actively involved in the process; they will help form the critical decisions that will shape the final project, and just as importantly, they'll be more invested in the outcome.

I'll reiterate: stakeholders not being actively involved makes it far less likely that you'll get the project over a useful finish line. The outcomes that matter to them will require prioritization and choices; while you can make those choices for them in theory, in practice you will often choose incorrectly. At the minimum, the stakeholders will need to be involved enough to define their goals at the beginning of the project and to give you your constraints. You can then have a clear idea of what you can and cannot do within the framework they lay out. Being forced to articulate those goals will also make them more invested in obtaining them, which will help if you need assistance in clearing obstacles.

From Listening to Determining the Work: A Missing Step

In the last chapter, you learned how to listen to stakeholders. Stakeholders tend to be able to describe what they care about and what their objectives and values are without much additional work. In contrast, they will often need help determining the problem space and articulating the *outcomes* they truly need. In this chapter, I'll show you how to help assist your stakeholders through the prioritization process.

Let's begin with the problem space.[7] To be sure that your work actually delivers the outcomes your stakeholder is looking for, it's critical to fully understand the problem you've been charged with. That means not only having a surface concept of your problem but understanding its edges and the systems it

---

7   The problem space is the landscape of the problem.

interacts with. Designers have long noticed that when you spend more time considering the problem space *before* charting out the solution space, or the world of potential solutions, you end up with better outcomes.

The problem space isn't the sum total of all aspects of the problem everywhere. *Your* problem space will be a specific subset of the overall problem that your stakeholder is considering. For example, the Centers for Medicare and Medicaid Services (CMS) has determined strategic priorities that are public. These strategic priorities—things like health equity, reducing drug costs, and improving nursing home oversight—operate as high-level goals or objectives but are not yet actionable. The problem space that my current company and teams work with is a smaller, more tangible piece of that high-level goal, something small enough for us to move the needle on.

Reducing drug costs isn't a thing that we as a company can influence directly; that's a task for Congress, to put legislation on the drug companies and limit their cost structure. But we *can* refocus the problem space to be more directly applicable to our work. For example, how could we give consumers better insight into drug prices and standardize drug costs across different health plans? Now we have a more defined problem to consider with our client.

As a note, even the decision to condense the problem space from (1) reducing drug costs to consumers to (2) giving consumers better insight into drug prices within health plans is *a strategic decision* that CMS made. Your stakeholders have also likely already done this level of thinking, but if not, it's worthwhile to begin with a larger solution space and to condense it as you begin to consider your problem together.

It is tempting to jump directly into the problem solving without having first studied the problem, and often stakeholders will ask for you to hastily execute on a solution. Even in these instances, it is worthwhile to take a step back to ensure you understand the problem the solution is meant to address. This ensures that you are working with the right problem and the right solution. Ideally, you will have the chance to do the work to define and work with the problem space, *then* define and ideate your solution.

Understanding Systems to Help Your Stakeholder

To round out your problem space, take the time to develop a clear and practical understanding of any systems that may be affecting your stakeholders' problem or priorities and any constraints driving their decisions that they may or may not have articulated.

For example, in the government space where I operate, understanding the full shape of a given problem *also* means understanding the surrounding policy, legislative timeline, and agency or project budget. Internal agency politics and external agency or government politics may also impact the work. In your context, you will find other details and influencing systems that affect your own work.

Be cautious though; not all of your constraints may be obvious at first glance! A solution that doesn't address a constraint won't be useful to either you or your stakeholder(s). If the project will fail if you don't deliver it in person on February 2nd, a delivery date of February 15th will not work *even if no one told you this hidden constraint to begin with*. It's worth taking the time to uncover all of the constraints that will affect your work.

Often people are not holding back information willfully or malignantly. The stakeholder may not yet have the details of constraints fully fleshed out and may need you to help do discovery with them or you may find that the information exists but hasn't been formally shared for whatever reason. Perhaps one stakeholder hasn't communicated with another. Regardless, helping your stakeholder means understanding the landscape you're operating within. (See Chapter Two for more details about what to listen for.)

Ask questions diplomatically so that you can get at what is most important and continue to ask them when appropriate as the project goes on. If a stakeholder asks you at the last minute for a feature that appears extraneous, you may be tempted to deprioritize it unless you understand why it came up when it did—perhaps an executive will not sign off without it. Context matters, and that context may shift during the course of the project. The best thing that you can do for your stakeholder is to deeply understand the situation and guide your stakeholder. If you and your team can't add "more," help them reprioritize according to their goals.

Understanding the situation does *not* mean never pushing back on your stakeholder, or blindingly accepting changes. If anything, once you know their point of view and their framing, you'll be in a better position to advocate for the things that are truly important. You'll be able to fit your work within the context that matters to deliver work with real impact.

When you understand the depth and shape of your stakeholder's problem and have a grasp of the systems and constraints that affect it, you can actually deliver solutions that matter.

Listen for Problem Details

Be sure that you can fully describe the following *from your stakeholder's perspective*:

- The specific problem you are solving, with any critical details.

- The systems that interact with that problem.
- All constraints you must work within, including timeline, budget, and interpersonal constraints.
- Any risks that you must address or ameliorate.
- What is most important in a solution.
- What values or outcomes your stakeholder will be judged against.
- The outcome(s) you will be held responsible for.
- Any additional factors for decision making.

Lastly, make a list of your assumptions and the things that you do not yet know but will need to know for future decisions. What data will you need to fill those gaps and make decisions?

While you may not choose to investigate or test every assumption on your list, explicitly defining your assumptions decreases your risk of unknown problems arising during the project. The same goes for gathering data with which to make decisions. When there isn't data to inform a decision, people may freeze and become unwilling to make a decision. They may also decide based on emotions or anecdotes and make a poor decision as a result.

The assumptions and missing data inherent in a problem are part of its problem space and should be explicitly stated. Then, once you've identified what you don't know, you can either study the situation further at the cost of additional time and effort, or you can put a stake in the ground while acknowledging it may be based on assumptions rather than data. Knowing that you made a specific decision without knowing X, Y, or Z means you may be far more likely to change your mind when new information arises.

Helping Stakeholders Prioritize

I've talked about the importance of focus, or having a clear direction and priorities to work against. Otherwise, you end up in the position that we did in the beginning of the chapter, ping-ponging from one initiative to the next. That is the fastest and easiest fail state for any given project. Maintaining focus is ongoing work.

When new circumstances arrive or when trade-offs become necessary, you may need to return to your stakeholders and guide them in a new round of prioritizing. I like to ask gentle questions from a subordinate position to help stakeholders articulate their goals. For example, I might say, "Help me understand...," or, "What's more important to you...?" or, "How does this fit into the larger goal?" When the decisions become complex, I use working sessions to lay out all of the data on the board together. Stakeholders can see the trade-offs with the implications for staffing, timeline, and resources all in one place. They can understand at a glance and decide between options.

I strongly recommend that you do not attempt to get multiple stakeholders to prioritize separately, but rather to get them all in a room to decide together. Yes, this may surface conflict and cause delays, but that conflict is best handled by the stakeholders as a group, rather than you attempting to satisfy each one individually.

Creating a good, structured working session with a clear agenda is most of the work in getting several stakeholders to align. Invite everyone who must weigh in for the decision to be final. Then lay out options, and ask the attendees to make the decision. They may struggle with the complexity, in which case you will need to offer a small number of clear options to choose from, or they may ask for some additional option, in which case you will tell them, "That sounds great," and ask which of your other priorities they would like you to drop.

If decision makers won't prioritize at all, you will need to suggest priorities yourself, explaining how and why, and ask for explicit sign-off. (If they push back, use the techniques I discuss in the How to Say No chapter.)

Sample Prioritization Working Session

1. Identify the affected stakeholders.
2. Clearly define the goal to be made in that specific working session and create a clear agenda.
3. Invite the stakeholders and any people involved in presenting the data to the meeting. Aim to present only what data is needed and reserve most of the time for discussion and prioritization. If you can get all of the affected stakeholders in the same room, in person is better. If not, Zoom is acceptable.
4. Research and assemble the data needed to make the decision.
5. Create visuals and product frameworks to make the data easy to understand.
6. Establish clear criteria for decision making in advance of the meeting. If needed, work with stakeholders to ensure they are weighted and prioritized appropriately. Include trade-off considerations.
7. On the date of the meeting, present the data.
8. Guide the stakeholders into making a solid, clear decision, taking trade-offs into account.

Each working session should not last more than 2 hours and should be focused toward that time. This often means only one big decision, such as deciding a project's priorities.

You may need to schedule multiple sessions if there are many decisions to work through. Consider that people will lose focus with longer meetings. For meetings about prioritization, you will often end the session with either (1) a list of initiatives ranked by which to do first or (2) a list of weighted criteria with which to make decisions moving forward.[8] Either way, you can now prioritize your work based on what's most important to your stakeholder(s) and their world.

Facilitating Answers

Stakeholders are often overwhelmed with inputs, impacting their ability to prioritize efficiently. Part of your role is to create the structure and grounding within which they can do this work more easily. The other part of your role is to surface any additional information or considerations in order to ensure they're deciding well. In helping them step back and articulate criteria for problem solving and prioritization, you enable them to function in their best selves.

Take care, however, not to add endless complexity without also sensemaking. An overwhelmed stakeholder—or worse, stakeholders—will not be served by information arranged haphazardly. Give them data that is directly tied to the decision they must make, and provide clear perspectives or paths forward. When in doubt, simpler is better.

An Example of How to Use a Working Session

I have found over the years that when setting up a new project it can be helpful to host a set of working sessions to define and

---

[8] A common and simple method is to reduce all of the criteria to two: cost and impact. You would then make all decisions going forward with respect to what path gives you the most impact per unit of cost. But your stakeholders may prefer "easy wins," positive press, or any other criteria. The point of the meeting is to elicit this answer clearly so that you can target your efforts appropriately.

establish the project. These sessions should be limited to at most a handful and run with as little preparation from stakeholders as possible.

For example, at one point Pitney Bowes experienced a reorg. Leaders decided to spin the R&D group into an innovation center tasked with running "opportunity forums" to develop ideas into roadmaps, similar to the project I discussed in the beginning of the chapter. Since none of us at Pitney Bowes had run an opportunity forum before, we hired a consultancy to help frame and run the first one. They gave us the format and methods for future forums freely as part of the engagement.

I observed the first forum and worked as part of the team for the second before being put in charge of the third and subsequent forums. The goal of these forums was to develop ideas and turn them into actionable roadmaps. The initial ones were successful in that they resulted in solid roadmaps. But the process the consulting company used to develop the roadmaps turned out to be far more work-intensive than was practical for our stakeholders, and the stakeholders were not executing on the roadmaps that were created.

Rather than having the stakeholders go through all of the intensive data-collecting and analyzing—steps recommended by the consulting company—I implemented a lighter-weight version. This both saved an immense amount of person-hours from my team, and it enabled the stakeholders to roll up their sleeves and engage directly with the work. I set up a handful of working sessions for the stakeholders and their direct reports to do the lighter-weight analysis and data work, and we went through a series of working sessions together.

Keep in mind that my team and I still did much of the heavy lifting to conduct background research. We brought in detailed information about trends, the user, and other topics germane to the discussion of each of the sessions. We brought in blank roadmaps to start populating. But in asking the stakeholders to be active participants in key decisions, we found that the projects moved faster internally. The assumptions we were working with were larger, and on occasion we'd have to reconsider decisions during the project (normally during the implementation segment, which I heard about from other teams internally). The speed with which we moved and the amount of buy-in we got from stakeholders more than made up for the difference in aggregate.

When the stakeholders participated in the creation of the project, they sheparded it through the system more actively from that point on. The working sessions were successful.

When You Can't Get the Stakeholder to Show Up

When you're facing a situation like I did with the innovation center, I recommend setting clear boundaries around stakeholder involvement. For example, I did not accept work internally without the stakeholder committing to attend the handful of working sessions. Holding that boundary led to much better work from everyone overall.

Occasionally, you may have a stakeholder who doesn't show up consistently, and you will, for one reason or another, have to complete the project on a timeline anyway. Stakeholders are often pulled in a variety of directions, and particularly as you earn more trust, you may find that they perceive your project as less emergent than others. So they may become less engaged or stop being engaged. If you can pause the project at this point until the stakeholder can reengage, this is the best practice. I strongly recommend that path. If you truly cannot pause the project until the stakeholder or stakeholders re-engage, do whatever you can asynchronously to press them towards decisions. Suggest a solution to the problem, and push for active agreement or disagreement on your plan to move forward. It's critical to get your stakeholder(s) to own the decision, even if that decision is to let you make all the decisions.

When you face stakeholders who don't want to be involved in general, lay out the risks of inaction: "Here is the plan, and here are the risks of me moving forward without your input, and if need be, here's how we ameliorate those risks." Do this face to face whenever possible, but if you have no other path forward, do so in an email.

The email should be framed in the following way: show that you have heard them and their challenges. Acknowledge that your asking for involvement causes issues for them because of their time needs or other challenges. Reflect back that you have heard them and understand their constraints. Suggest that you move forward with you making decisions (or another path), but warn them of the challenges involved. Ask them to confirm that they are okay with those trade-offs with a simple yes or no reply.

Again, however, holding boundaries to not begin work or to not continue work until they can re-engage is far preferable.

How to Apply This Chapter

I have seen many good projects with good technical work fail on a large scale because of assumptions. For example, an agency might build an online application without the ability to save intermediate steps. If more than half of its users need to return several times after getting additional information, the application is preventing the agency from providing services effectively. That assumption would kill the project, and no one would know until the end.

In order to protect your own work, take a moment and go through the formal assumptions-mapping exercise below. Formally identifying your assumptions and unknowns helps both you and your stakeholder solve problems and reach outcomes more effectively. Not every assumption or gap in knowledge has to be researched immediately—some can exist for a longer period of time comfortably. But all assumptions *must* be identified.

First by yourself and then with your stakeholders or coworkers, go through your project and make a note of:

- Any assumptions you have made about the project, its constituents (customers, users, beneficiaries), or how the ultimate products or services must be delivered
- Any other assumptions about the project or the stakeholders that could affect the outcomes of the project, especially any that may imperil your results if not true

Similarly, list anything you do not know that could affect the outcomes of the project

I like to use a version of the template below to get me started. Be sure to add additional rows to customize the template to your specific technical specialty and project.

When you are done listing the assumptions and unknowns (being sure to add additional rows), identify the pieces of information that you know but cannot back up with data. These too are assumptions and should be coded as such.

Now, color code each assumption and unknown into one of the following categories:

- *Must* be investigated or researched now
- *Likely* needs to be investigated before important decisions or milestones

	What we know and how we know it	What we assume and why we assume it	What we don't know and why we need to know it
Users			
Context of use			
Impact on the overall ecosystem			
Risks			

- *Should* be watched carefully but needs no additional action
- *Can* be ignored for now

Then act accordingly. Research to get the information you need to move forward now and in the future. Then be open to revisiting assumptions and getting additional information as you continue to work.

No one can research everything that may affect a project, but making assumptions and unknowns explicit is critical work. It improves design and user decisions, and it decreases risk. By honestly grappling with assumptions with your stakeholder and identifying where decisions are made without all of the information, you improve the quality of your project and your work. You also make the *outcomes* you deliver far more likely.

Two-Minute Summary

Good work isn't enough. It has to be the right work, to solve the right problem in the right context, to deliver the right outcomes.

- Study your problem space, and work with your stakeholders to determine the piece of the problem you will focus on.
- Understand the systems and constraints around the problem as well as the outcomes needed.
- List the assumptions and data you will need for decision making.
- Help your stakeholders prioritize at the beginning of the project and periodically as new changes arise.
- When dealing with multiple stakeholders, get them into a room for a working session or sessions.
- Doing all of this positions your work for the best results and the most impact.

CHAPTER FIVE

SAYING NO WITHOUT SAYING NO

If you guide your stakeholders through trade-offs diplomatically and with integrity, you won't have to tell them no very often. When you do, here's how to handle it with integrity in a way that maintains relationships.

A FEW YEARS AGO, I WORKED WITH A CLIENT ON A PUBLIC WEB portal designed to allow organizations to apply for grant funding. I had built a solid working relationship with my primary stakeholder for this project and understood her goals and priorities.

We were tasked with building a form that would allow the agency to respond in a timely manner to applications and would interface smoothly with their legacy systems. This basically meant that the data coming from the form had to be clean and accurate. The stakeholder asked for many changes to the form and for additional fields and options to be added to the point the form became confusing.

The designers were frustrated and rightly concerned about a terrible user experience. However, based on previous interactions with my stakeholder, I knew that a plea for a better user experience would not resonate with her. Instead, I took a different approach. "If we make this change, it puts your data at risk," I told her. "This form is one that people are required to use. They will use it regardless, but if it's confusing they will not fill it out properly, and you will get bad data you'll need to spend a lot of person-hours cleaning. The more clear the form is, the fewer mistakes people will make filling it out." You'll notice at no point in the conversation did I use the word "no." Instead, I gently walked her through why the change would harm her most important priority.

Saying No Without Saying No

Managing a relationship with a stakeholder doesn't mean you always agree to everything they ask. You have built expertise over many years, and you will need to use that expertise and your professional judgment to deliver excellent work in the service of your stakeholder's goals. Because of this reality, you will often hit points in a project where saying yes to your stakeholder will not lead to a good outcome. But if you handle the conversation well, you will almost never need to tell them no outright.

As you approach these conversations, consider yourself a trusted advisor helping your stakeholder choose the path to their stated goals. Since you have listened and helped your stakeholder prioritize as part of your earlier work, you know what is important to them. When they ask for something that may impact those goals, you can point back to what was previously said: "Great! Tell me more. Is this more important than [the other priority]?" "Is this worth the impact on [this other thing]?" By knowing their priorities and outcomes, you are able to help them consider what they are asking for in the context of other work and goals.

If necessary, you may also need to help them understand other stakeholders' points of view. Walk them through the trade-offs of potential changes and make the impact on their priorities clear. If you do this with care and respect, they will normally engage in a thoughtful dialog that clarifies next steps.

Your Instinct May Be to Say Yes Too Quickly

A civil engineer friend of mine oversees three teams of people working at a large company. He recently told me about problems they were having with two stakeholders at a client organization. The first, who we'll call Marcus, is an executive with strong opinions and internal "pull" who exerts his opinions into project decisions on a regular basis, often to the exclusion of the agreed-upon plan. He causes chaos when he is not read into decisions, even though the project is not in his reporting line. Nonetheless the teams got used to copying him on updates and soliciting his input. The second stakeholder, who we'll call Natasha, is the senior manager who is responsible for delivering the goals the organization wants from the project. She is level-headed and competent but isn't someone who makes waves. Over the course of several weeks, two separate senior executives have made it clear that she is the decision maker with input from two other stakeholders I won't name here. Marcus' opinion should not be driving the work.

My civil engineer friend expressed deep frustration at how hard it was for his teams to change their behavior. They still go to Marcus, rather than Natasha, to get approval before proceeding, even though everyone had received clear direction to do the opposite. "Why is this so hard?" he complained to me. "We're all grown professionals, but we're acting like we're twelve." When asked, two separate members of the teams in question said they didn't like telling Marcus no, even by implication.

Many of us are raised to make people happy. We want to do a good job so our parents, our teacher, or our boss is pleased.

Even as full-fledged adults, we as humans are social creatures. We still want to make connections with others and keep those connections smooth. We may instinctively want to agree to what a stakeholder is asking for so that we can maintain a pleasant relationship. It feels bad to disagree. A knee-jerk yes, though, can often lead to negative long-term results.

Saying yes to everything means you'll agree to outcomes that you will ultimately be unable to deliver. The anger and disappointment on the back end will be far worse than the temporary irritation of a quick no. That is equally true, by the way, of any normal boundaries you will need to hold with stakeholders, such as refusing to do unethical actions or doing what's right for your company when dealing with an outside client. A prompt and clear statement of what you can and cannot do will nearly always land better than a wishy-washy yes that you walk back.

I'm a big proponent of keeping your stakeholder happy, and in fact I recommend specific ways to do that in every chapter. Keeping them happy, however, does *not* mean always saying yes. In fact, if saying yes means they don't get what they want and need long-term, yes is guaranteed to make them *un*happy.

If you are a person who is tempted to say yes too quickly, consider that you will make your stakeholder far *more* unhappy by agreeing to something you cannot ultimately do.

Don't Rush to No

While some people have to fight their instinct to people please, others have a natural instinct for no. This too is important to moderate. If you constantly question stakeholders, they can feel frustrated by you and even start to expect that you will be negative about everything. Rather than feeling blocked, you want your stakeholder to feel an energy of partnership with you.

If you have an ongoing tendency to want to say no outright or to tell the stakeholder that something is a bad idea, see that as an opportunity to reflect: Why don't you like the situation, exactly? Is it about you and your desires in the situation, or is there something about the situation that needs to be addressed in order to do good work?

For example, if you are inclined to say that something shouldn't be done because there's not time for it, you are in a position to talk with your stakeholder about time constraints. You can make a chart that shows the number of people, the amount of work, and what can be done and make your case as to why the new addition is unwise. Your initial instinct was good, but you will need to deliver the information in a way that makes sense to your stakeholder, and act as their advisor rather than their blocker. The same goes for any other situation in which there are trade-offs.

How then should you approach your stakeholder in these high-stakes conversations?

The Ethics of Refusal

In a recent conference I attended, Dustin Kiskaddon—a VP of Experience Research at Chase who is also a former tattoo artist—gave a lightning talk about the ethics of refusal. He talked about his experience when people came into the shop wanting a tattoo on their face. To say yes was to almost certainly consign the client to major regret in the future. To say no would make them angry in the moment. It felt like a no-win situation.

Kiskaddon ultimately learned to handle that kind of request gently. He felt ethically obligated to refuse, but the method ended up looking more like redirection. "I don't think that design is going to work on your face, but what if we put it here?" He would suggest an alternate plan that would take the spirit of what they were asking for and apply it to a location less likely to lead to regret.

In the lightning talk, Kiskaddon extended this approach to business. He said, "Think of the client's idea as a shitty first draft, one that needs refinement and editing." He recommended creating a culture of decision making where refusal is done in three steps, RAD. (1) Read the situation, (2) align with the stakeholder, and (3) display your expertise.

Show Respect for Their Perspective

Before responding to any request, make sure that you understand what your stakeholder is asking for specifically. Respectfully ask questions to clarify that understanding, paying close attention to the *why* and the desired outcome. Then, once you understand, take a moment. Consider if what they want can be accomplished within the scope of their priorities. It may be that what they want is more possible than you'd originally thought.

If you still feel the need for more discussion after gaining this information, show respect for your stakeholder by demonstrating your understanding of what they want in positive terms. Articulate the position they are in and what they are trying to do, using their words if possible: "You are facing pressure to do X, Y, and Z, and so…." Then you can present the challenges and trade-offs. If there are other stakeholders in the mix who have given you different feedback, report what they have said. (You may need to schedule a working session to resolve conflicts between your stakeholders.)

Based on your relationship with your single stakeholder and your situation, you will handle the rest of the conversation with one of two tactics. Either (1) you'll guide them towards better options for achieving their goals, or (2) you'll guide them towards what has to be given up to have this new thing. In both cases, the conversation will turn toward trade-offs. Rather than making promises you cannot keep or blocking them entirely, you show respect by giving data for decision making.

Take care with your approach *and* your tone of voice so that you demonstrate respect in the details. The conversation should come from the frame of "here are the ways in which I can help you get to your big-picture goals" *not* "this is a terrible idea and you can't do it," even if the latter only comes across in implication. Your role is to help your stakeholder achieve their goals, and demonstrating respect buys you space to make your case *well*.

The New Initiative

The trade-offs conversation looks different for different circumstances. But I will walk you through an example situation, with the exact words I would use, to illustrate how the conversation *might* work. Be sure to put the principles into the words that feel authentic to you, and adapt the approach to the situation and to the person you're talking to. (You should hopefully know how to do this for your specific stakeholder already, based on listening. When in doubt, though, use direct communication with direct people and polite deference with those who communicate indirectly until you have updated information.)

Let's take an example in which the client had agreed to the priorities for the team and signed off on them six weeks ago. Today, they arrive with a new initiative from the executive offices. They tell you that the new work is absolutely critical and that it should be done ASAP.

Begin by asking questions, such as:

- "Please tell me more about this initiative. I want to make sure I fully understand it. Why is this a priority now?"
- "What outcomes are the executives looking for?"
- "What is success here? What is failure?"

Once you fully understand what is being asked, take a moment to think through the challenges, and respond with respect:

"Thank you. I see why this is so important. We can absolutely get right on it. However, in order to give it the attention it deserves, the team is going to have to delay [X, Y, and Z.]"

If the stakeholder is not pleased with this idea and says that these delays are not acceptable, respond by suggesting we delay other items A, B, and C. Often stakeholders will sign off on delays smoothly.

If the client insists that nothing can be delayed, take a moment, and then respond respectfully:

"I understand how important all of these are. I am concerned that because of how important they are, we need to ensure they have the right time and resources to be done correctly. In order to get them all done on the original timeline, I will need additional resources. Specifically, I'll need 3 additional people at a cost of $X."

You can then go on to give a full explanation of how resources will be used to support their goals, and explain all trade-offs in terms that matter *to them,* not to your team, so that the stakeholder fully understands what is being asked. Ninety-five percent of the time, the conversation will stop here. For that last, particularly difficult stakeholder, you should warn and then document:

> "I understand. I need you to be aware that the risks of moving forward 'as is' are [exact risks]. I am going to put that in our decision sheet and in our risk matrix so we know these are documented moving forward."

If the stakeholder remains resistant to making trade-off decisions, you can then lay out the situation in writing to whatever stakeholders you have internally, along with a warning of the potential risks. Somewhere, somebody needs to know what may happen and that you've warned the client.

Always approach the conversation with the attitude that their request can be done, even if it requires adjustments. In general I may or may not remind the stakeholder of their priorities, but that information is always top of mind for me. It establishes whether there is room to fit additional work and what trade-offs may need to happen. It also allows me to reference their priorities as we discuss the impact of changes.

Documenting the Conversation

I recommend documenting every trade-off conversation in a follow-up email you send to your stakeholder. Don't document so that you can throw their agreement in their face later, but rather do it to clarify understanding and to build leverage for future difficult conversations. Documentation can be helpful to clarify to all parties what was agreed to, since people can often leave verbal conversations with very different understandings of decisions. By writing out the decision and ensuring your stakeholder agrees that the document accurately reflects their understanding, you give the stakeholder an opportunity to disagree *before* it causes wasted effort. Don't rely on "posted meeting notes" to serve as a shortcut for this kind of agreement on decisions. Instead, explicitly document X, Y, or Z, and have someone sign off or clarify what they meant instead.

This will not prevent stakeholders from changing their minds—but if a shift in direction will require trade-offs, you will be able to reference the earlier decision and thought process. That will help you work through those trade-offs with your stakeholders and help them understand those challenges as they prioritize.

Documentation also serves as protection for you if the worst case happens. Written proof that someone agreed is useful to limit damage, particularly if you warned them explicitly about what could happen. If then that thing were to happen, it is not as easy for your stakeholder to lay the blame on your shoulders.

Keep in mind that not making a decision or taking action is also a decision and will lead to outcomes. You should also document when a stakeholder has not committed to a course of action.

Example Questions

Since every situation and conversation is slightly different, I'm giving you a list of additional questions to consider asking:

- You've said [this bigger objective] is important. Do you want us to deprioritize that objective in favor of this new one?
- Is this going to the top of the stack or the bottom of the stack?
- We could absolutely switch our effort to this. It's going to mean X, Y, and Z. Are you okay with that?

- Help me figure this out. Given our timeline, I do not think we can do everything. What should I deprioritize to get this done? (You may need to provide a list of things already prioritized.)
- I hear that you want these things for this reason. I am concerned about this potential outcome that might happen as a result. Does that worry you?
- Can I have more resources? Or more time?

Don't Let Them Wear You Down

No matter how forceful your stakeholder is, I strongly recommend that you avoid agreeing to something that you can't actually do. If you're forced to agree to something impossible, I recommend escalating to your boss or theirs to get ahead of the situation.

By far the biggest challenge I see in the teams that report to me on the topic of this chapter is resisting stakeholders who try to steamroll them here. Yes, some stakeholders are forceful in their opinions, and many are highly sensitive to perceived power. You are there to deliver for that stakeholder, and that power differential is real. Despite this, if you say yes to something you cannot deliver, you are actually not doing your job.

Saying yes in that circumstance does not benefit the stakeholder, and it does not benefit you. It also sets up a bad situation for your company, and your stakeholder's insistence does not change that. Generally if you have put in the time to build a solid working relationship as I have described up to this point, you will have earned yourself the room to bring up trade-offs and priority shifts. You will be given the forum to discuss why something is impossible, and saying no without saying no will not be as challenging as you might imagine. If anything, putting yourself into the role of advisor will *help* you with your stakeholder in the long term.

Bring the conversation back to their larger goal. "If you do X, this is why I believe it will not get you to Y." Frame the risks, the timing, and the resources in terms that matter to them, and they will nearly always respond well. (We'll return to the question of truly difficult stakeholders and how to handle them in Chapter Seven.)

Of course sometimes you will simply have to do the thing anyway, even if you feel it is ill-advised.

Is It Worth the Battle?

When dealing with stakeholders—or really, anyone—there will be cases in which it is easier to do the thing rather than to fight about it. Do you have room in your schedule to add the new thing without negative impact? If so, you will likely just want to do it, even if the thing itself is unpleasant. It's not worth the hit to your relationship with your stakeholder to fight back.

I'll give an example from my personal life to illustrate the point. I am on a nonprofit board with some very strong-willed people. One is a lawyer known for being strong-willed and persistent. In her day job, those traits are extremely beneficial, but they can also cause conflict in other contexts.

In a recent conversation about a business issue, she decided that we had to resolve a problem by making a phone call, and she felt I would get better results from calling than she would. I'm a professional and good on the phone, but I felt for various reasons that the outcome of this phone call would be poor. I didn't want to do it. But I knew she had made up her mind and would nag me until it was done. So I picked up the phone and called because it was easier than fighting her. As expected, the call ended up being a waste of time, and we had to resolve the issue in writing.

I have seen the same dynamic in corporate America. Sometimes people are so insistent on a particular course of action that it changes the dynamic. You then must decide whether it's worth redirecting them or whether you should warn them once or twice and then just do it (with documentation). Sometimes people have to see things fail before they will listen.

If your stakeholder is in that position and you are being asked to do something you know will turn out badly, have the discussion about why it's the wrong course of action. If they still insist, protect yourself, most likely by warning them in writing. You may choose to escalate depending on circumstance; you may not. If the action is not unethical or dangerous in some way, you may then have to bite the bullet. You are there to deliver for the stakeholder, and sometimes that means doing things that will fail.

You may not know why they are so insistent on doing something a particular way. They may not tell you, and you should not be pestering them incessantly in any case. Sometimes they have been given clear direction from on high and *must* follow that direction to keep their jobs. Choose your battles, and choose the ones you can win.

In general if your stakeholder has pushed back more than once and you have presented the trade-offs, don't push back again unless lives are on the line.

Of course your approach to stakeholders should always be that this path will not deliver their goals, not that this path is a bad idea.

Framing Trade-Offs

When I teach teams to have conversations with stakeholders, I often get questions about how to frame trade-offs appropriately. First, the trade-offs should always be presented in the stakeholder's terms. In the case of the client who did not care about user experience but *did* care about data, the correct framing was "If we add more fields to the form, our concern is that it will become confusing and that users will input data with many more mistakes from the confusion." The framing should *not* be, "If we add more fields to the form, the user experience will be poor." Paying attention to your stakeholder's goals and values means that you will know how best to approach the discussion.

As a note, one of the most important functions of your job in this relationship is to deliver *outcomes* rather than partial results. Twelve half-completed features are less useful than one complete one, regardless of the priority of each. Doing sixteen small tasks that add up to nothing is less useful than providing one larger result that leads to the stakeholder's goals. Guide your stakeholder to focus and decide on clear paths forward that get them to entire, completed outcomes. The trade-off discussion should help facilitate these decisions.

I do recommend that you use visuals to illustrate information clearly in these discussions. Visuals help stakeholders get a big-picture view of the decisions to be made and help them interact with data in a more useful, granular fashion.

If Your Stakeholder Won't Make Decisions

I have found over the years that stakeholders are normally happy to work through decisions and priorities, especially if you get all influencing parties in the same room. The more that you can give them the structure and context they need to make the decision, the easier the process will be for everyone.

Occasionally, you will find a stakeholder who truly will not prioritize or make a critical decision that must be made. They will not participate no matter how much you prompt. In that case, you will need to come back to them with a list of priorities that you recommend and get them to sign off. In this case, as with all other potentially tricky moments in the project, document what happens carefully.

Of course no matter how carefully and well you decide, you may have to adjust again as the world and your information changes. Work is always changing as are priorities, but you can decide and re-decide in positive and productive directions.

The Counterproductive Ask

Most situations with stakeholders can be resolved with a trade-off or priorities discussion. Occasionally, though, when a stakeholder is asking for something that will actively prevent you from reaching their goals, you will have to guide their thinking in a different way.

When you get a counterproductive ask, it's tempting to immediately push back. Instead, begin with a question about their desired outcomes. You are listening to hear the *why* behind the *what*, as you'll use it later in the conversation. The questions will also force your stakeholder to consider their larger purpose. They may or may not have put it into words yet, even in their own mind.

Here's how I would ask the outcomes question; adapt the approach to your words and to the person you're talking to:

> "Please tell me what outcomes you are looking for. If this is successful, what will success look like?"

Asking this question will tend to make the stakeholder pause to think, which will also create space for you to consider their words and priorities more deeply along with the consequences of what they're proposing.

1. After you fully understand the immediate outcome, consider whether the proposed thing will actually lead to that goal.

   THEN

2. If the outcome is achievable with the proposed thing, ask yourself if it will be counterproductive to their larger priorities.
   - If not, you may need to start the trade-offs conversation from earlier in the chapter.
   - If it is indeed counterproductive, say something like this:

   "I understand why that is important. Can you help me understand how this fits into X goal we have discussed [in this time frame]? As important as it is, this seems like it will distract [or prevent] us from achieving X. Has there been a change in focus that we should document?"[9]

3. If the proposed thing won't actually lead to the stakeholder's goal, say something like the following:

   "I understand why that is important, and I want to make sure I/we help you succeed. Can we talk about whether there are other ways to reach that goal? I am concerned that this may not get you there because of

---

[9] "Document" is a word designed to give your stakeholder pause here, to have them stop and consider their own intentions. Documentation provides protection for you if you must move forward to do something against your better judgment. It can also slow down bad decisions in a client relationship or in a bureaucratic culture where the stakeholder would then become concerned about their exposure to judgment from others. Given the strength of the word, though, you should take care to use it out loud only where truly needed.

X, Y, and Z. However, if we do Plan B, it could achieve your goal by way of C. But maybe there is something I am not understanding, and I would like to work with you to ensure we are doing what you need."

Here you are trying to establish a feeling of collaboration. You want the stakeholder to feel like you and they are on the same team trying to reach their goal. So if you can't think of Plan B on the spot, start a discussion:

"Let's talk through how we could reach your goal by another path."

Presenting Stakeholders with Negative Information

Sometimes you will not know how a given plan impacts your stakeholder's priorities until much later in the project, or you will initially think you can deliver the new ask *and* the old outcome in the same amount of time and then discover that you cannot. The way to approach the stakeholder in both cases is similar to the trade-offs conversation I scripted earlier.

New information inevitably arises; when you receive it, the important part is to go to your stakeholder promptly with an accurate assessment. For example, at the time I was there, Pitney Bowes staffed mail rooms and file rooms in addition to supplying hardware. Leadership decided to institute Six Sigma, making managers more efficient in how they used their time. They sent researchers out to discover the opportunities to improve efficiency in the staffed mail and file rooms.

Unfortunately, what we learned on the ground actively contradicted the assumptions of the project. The managers weren't efficient for a simple reason: their jobs were interruption driven. Being responsive to clients—a key determination of success—actively required them to be interrupted constantly. Any program we instituted to make their work more efficient would also make them less responsive and cost Pitney Bowes work. We had to go back to the stakeholder who had sent us and tell him what we had learned. Based on the data and trade-offs, the stakeholder decided to give up on the initiative. It was a challenging day, but by communicating clearly and promptly, we were able to serve the needs of our stakeholder even when what he wanted wasn't possible.

Owning Up to Your Mistakes

In the same way as delivering bad news, it's also important to promptly and clearly own up to your mistakes. When you own up to your responsibility for how something came out, you hold yourself accountable. Accountability builds trust.

In general if you make a mistake that impacts the project significantly and that cannot be easily fixed, don't wait to be found out; bring the issue up yourself. Take responsibility for what has happened, and propose a path forward. Don't try to excuse the mistake or explain it away as if you were somehow the good guy. Stakeholders aren't dumb, and the verbal tap-dance will only make you seem dishonest.

That is not to say that you should own other peoples' mistakes. We've had instances where another vendor made a mistake, and an agency stakeholder came to us to fix it because they trusted us. If it was our mistake, they knew we would fix it. Unfortunately, we didn't have access to that part of the project, and we didn't take on responsibility for fixing an error that wasn't ours.

On the other hand, if your team makes a mistake, acknowledge that mistake gracefully. For example, we had a new manager come in to a program with a section currently in chaos. A stakeholder on the client side asked him, "Who's responsible for this?" He had been there a week, and it would have been easy to demure. Instead, he responded, "I am the manager. I am responsible. I am happy to address the issue with you now." He didn't throw anyone under the bus or name names, but rather took full responsibility and worked towards a solution immediately.

When you own up to your mistakes or your team's mistakes, when you fix them and move forward, you build deep relationships of trust. You get more leverage to speak in the future, and you get more forgiveness when you mess up again.

When Two Instructions Contradict

When dealing with stakeholders, it's not uncommon to receive mutually-contradictory instructions. Resolving the conflict between those instructions doesn't always require *trade-offs* per se, but it *does* require a hard conversation. I'll illustrate the approach using a specific recent example from my work.

In a recent project, the software team was using a task management ticketing system to both track our work and to provide the client with visibility to that work. Our stakeholder told us to only ticket our own staff. However, during one initiative the client stakeholder chided us for not assigning tickets to one of his direct reports (which was literally what he had told us not to do). The team lead gently pulled the stakeholder aside and asked about the change.

Here is how I approach a conversation where I need to resolve the conflicting information in a situation where it is literally impossible to do both. I begin by reminding the stakeholder that I also want to make the relationship work for their goals:

> "Of course, you know that our job is to partner with you, and we want to make things work in a way that supports you the best."

Then I go into the specifics of the contradiction and ask for resolution:

> "You've asked us to add your people as owners of specific tickets. Our concern is that in the past you have said explicitly not to add them so that we are not perceived to be assigning work as we are supporting you. Since that guidance is also in the contract, let's work this out and get everything in writing about what your expectations are."

Often, I will also try to clarify *why* they're asking for the change:

> "What's your end goal here with the change? How can we help you accomplish that?"

Once we're able to talk through the issue, I can help guide the stakeholder into a path that will suit both sets of goals.

After much discussion, in this situation the team resolved the question successfully in favor of using the tickets. It created more ease of use and faster tracking of responsibility, and the client resolved their concern about assigning work through a different process change.

Dealing with Multiple Stakeholders

You will often face situations where several stakeholders are influencing your project, often in different directions. When two or more people in power want mutually exclusive things, getting them in a room is normally the best move. Let them work out between themselves how to reprioritize and move forward.

Help facilitate if needed:

> "I know you both are heavily invested in this, and I'd really like a working session with the two of you to understand how we can best meet all of your needs."

If you are confident in your relationship with both stakeholders, it may be politic to be more forthright:

> "I'm getting conflicting information, and it's possible I'm misunderstanding. I wanted to ask the questions in the right place so that you both could help me sort this out."

If you are unsure of your relationship, however, it's best to be careful with your words. The implication with "conflicting information" is that someone is wrong, and many stakeholders will take that badly. If you know yours will not, that can be a more direct path.

When You *Must* Say No

Very rarely, a stakeholder will ask you to do something that is dangerous, unethical, or illegal in some way. Even in this circumstance, it's important to treat your stakeholder with respect. Don't come back with a direct accusation: "You're asking me to do something illegal." Approach the situation instead with gentleness, with an assumption that they don't realize the problem. Don't use words that can be perceived as blaming, as if they were stupid or wrong. Instead, act as their advisor, letting them know new information.

The same goes when telling a stakeholder that something is truly impossible. Don't dismiss the stakeholder or act as if they should already know. Enlighten them gently, and help them understand the reality and how to get to their goals by another path.

Balancing Your Own Priorities

Finally, there is one last kind of no I want to address. Throughout this chapter, I have been telling you how to redirect the stakeholder towards their goals. I have been assuming that you personally are leaning into work and delivering against the projects you have been assigned. That will be true the vast majority of the time. Sometimes, however, you may decide that you have family priorities that must take precedence. For example, if you cannot work over Yom Kippur or Christmas or you must prioritize a specific family trip, do so honestly and respectfully, being willing to take the consequences. Balance your own priorities.

No matter how respectfully you push back on your stakeholder in this way, it *will* affect the relationship. It may affect your pay or your promotion. If you are being put between a rock and a hard place repeatedly, you may decide to exit the situation in favor of finding a new job. How to manage your work-life balance and your own life priorities is beyond the scope of this book, but it's worth considering carefully.

Consider Your Context

If you find yourself using the information in this chapter frequently, redirecting your stakeholder over and over or outright saying no often, that should serve as a red flag. Ask yourself *why*. In the same way, if you're saying yes to everything and you're struggling, you may have a problem, or you're about to have a problem where you can't deliver. Either way, something is wrong with the relationship. You might have a difficult stakeholder (see Chapter Seven), or you might need to work on repairing the relationship by going back to the practice of one-on-ones and listening.

If you're constantly feeling pressured or redirected or feeling like you're not actually achieving anything, take it as a sign. Work needs to be done with your stakeholders to repair the relationship; refocus your tactics and conversations on repairing and on advising them on what is likely to get them to their outcomes.

Becoming an Advisor

The basic principle will serve you throughout your career with stakeholders: try not to fall into the role of order taker, rather see yourself as an advisor. Help the stakeholder get to their actual goals rather than just the thing they asked for on a Tuesday.

Your job is to help navigate the stakeholder towards the outcomes they want and need, helping them understand what is possible, realistic, and likely. That way, choices can be made explicitly, and the stakeholder will be comfortable with the consequences. Otherwise, choices will be made by reality in a way that disappoints everyone. The difficult conversations serve you and your stakeholder alike.

Handle your conversations well, and you won't often have to tell your stakeholder no. You will be able to show them the respect of their position, and the respect they deserve for the expertise and perspective they bring to the table. By communicating and showing you're there to support their goals, you also earn trust to support an even more solid relationship in the future. You will earn the position of advisor and the person they trust to deliver for them.

That does not, in any way, mean that you cannot argue for your side. When I'm with my own boss, I will lay out the information and argue which path we should take. Making my case, even forcefully, is an active gesture of respect for her intelligence and competence. I know she wants to hear outside perspectives, as do I, and we have the relationship trust needed to support the forcefulness. She also knows that I will back up her decision once it is made and follow it with alacrity and consistency.

How to Apply This Chapter

Imagine a conversation with a stakeholder who is asking for something you strongly suspect they will regret later. Use Dustin Kiskaddon's model from earlier in the chapter (RAD) to plan out how you will say no without saying no.

Include the following sections to your soft refusal:

- **Read the situation,** or understand what they are asking for.
- **Align with the stakeholder,** or demonstrate you are on their side.
- **Display your expertise,** and guide them towards a better solution.

Two-Minute Summary

You may not always be able to say yes, but if you handle conversations well, you will almost never have to tell your stakeholder no.

- For many people the natural instinct is yes, and for others the instinct is no. Be careful of either tendency, and instead work to discuss trade-offs.
- Every conversation with a stakeholder should begin and end with respect.
- Most issues can be resolved with the trade-off conversation, but some may require you to guide your stakeholder in making (sometimes complex) decisions about priorities.
- Document all decisions carefully.
- Other sensitive conversations include those to resolve mutually-contradictory guidance and two opposing stakeholders.
- For the rare times when you will have to say no outright, such when you are asked to do something illegal or unethical or something that is truly impossible, handle the explanation gently.
- See yourself as an advisor, not an order taker.

CHAPTER SIX

PRESENTING YOUR WORK EFFECTIVELY

Now that you've done your work well, how do you present it to your stakeholder so they will listen and (hopefully) act?

A FEW YEARS AGO I WAS ASKED TO PRESENT MY WORK AT MY business unit's quarterly meeting with the C-Suite at Pitney Bowes. I had prepared a PowerPoint that explained the results of the research I was doing with small businesses, which were more than 80 percent of the company's client base. Most of their revenue came from large businesses, but there was a growing recognition that they might be able to grow revenue with small businesses.

I initiated a research program to understand how Pitney Bowes could support small businesses better and earn more revenue. Up until that point, the company had only considered these businesses in terms of the volume of mail they sent. I did new research on the problem as well as consolidating several years of existing research. After a review of all of the data, I was proposing new segmentation so that each type of small business could be offered more tailored solutions.

The day of the quarterly review meeting arrived, and the earlier presentations ran longer than expected. As we approached the end of the meeting, it was clear that my 15 minutes would not be available. The CEO said, "We'll tee you up for next quarter," but we had not quite run out of time yet.

"Can I have two minutes to summarize?" I asked.

The CEO agreed. I jumped to my last slide, emphasizing the key message: the company needed to look at small businesses in a different way. While I didn't have enough time to explain how or why, it was enough to plant a seed. Not long after, the company formed a larger initiative to segment small businesses for marketing purposes—what I had suggested—and I was asked to join.

More than once I've faced a similar situation. I always ask to give the salient points of my talk in literally two minutes, and I'm nearly always allowed to speak. I make one point with supporting details and display one slide. Frequently my point is heard well enough to impact decisions. The stakeholders often choose to invite me back. They've learned to trust my sense of what is important, and so my work earns impact.

Of course, it wasn't always this way for me.

Presentations That Got Ignored

Like many researchers, my background is in academia where I got a PhD in Anthropology before moving to industry. While many of the skills I learned—project management, interviewing, and data analysis for example—were directly helpful to my career in industry, others became counterproductive to success in my new world. I've since heard the same from technically-trained colleagues in other specialties.

Presentations are one of the biggest key differences between how I was trained technically and what the business world requires. In academia, presentations prove authority through detail and methodology, delivering insights and analyses for a technically-sophisticated audience to incorporate into their own work. Sometimes the presentations will conclude with directions for future research, but rarely do they provide recommendations or applications. Unfortunately, this structure does not provide what is needed to make this work impactful outside academia.

I discovered this truth the hard way. Early in my career, I made many presentations explaining my process and highlighting what I learned. They were completely ignored. I have since attended a wide variety of presentations, both inside and outside my specialty, with the same structure, that led to the same result. I realized after some time that I too would have likely ignored these presentations.

In order to have an impact, by which I mean effectively contributing to decision-making or other actions, you will have to do more than explain what you learned or what you did. It's all too easy to put together a guide, show a powerful video, or make an argument that in the moment seems to convince or wow the audience and then to feel that you have done enough. But to make a real impact on a business audience, *how* you present the work matters.

In the rest of the chapter, I will teach you the approach I have built for my own career. Much of it is common sense. When you connect the dots between the data and potential decisions, actions, and outcomes, the data has more impact. The meaning and the application—the very things that technical people are discouraged from describing—become the centerpiece of a business presentation with staying power.

To influence your stakeholders, create deliverables and presentations that tell the *story* of your data; focus on the decisions, actions, and outcomes that are needed. The story and the connections will create impact.

Making Them Care

Researchers often spend a great deal of time trying to get stakeholders to have empathy for users. The common refrain I hear is, "If they only understood how bad it is, they'd make it better." The complaint is especially frequent in my area of civic tech, where admittedly social and technological systems can be broken and change can be frustratingly slow. But the problem with the lament is the hidden assumptions embedded within it.

The two incorrect assumptions are (1) that others are lacking in knowledge and (2) that bringing the knowledge will do most of the work of solving the problem. Neither is a helpful assumption. Often stakeholders do know and do care, but they may not know the full extent of problems or exactly where and why they happen—and this is where we can help. But defining the problem, bringing them knowledge of the problem, is unlikely to be enough on its own.

The latter fallacy is unfortunately common for technical people. They often believe firmly in the Charles Kettering statement: "A problem well defined is half solved." Bringing a problem to light and proposing ideas can solve technical problems, often easily. But problems that are easy to solve don't persist. Stakeholders are often dealing with interlocking systems of issues with difficult-to-resolve trade-offs and complications. Giving them data divorced from decisions, even data about a specific problem, won't have the same impact as a concrete recommendation that they can implement today.

As Georgia Tech professor Carl DiSalvo put it in a presentation I heard a couple of years ago, we need to think about "how... we articulate the problem in such a way that it is tractable and solvable by the people who can solve it." In other words, the process of how we *frame* a given problem can make the difference between whether the person in the position to solve that problem can solve it and whether or not they care enough to try. Telling your stakeholder about a bad user experience may not make a difference if that is not a problem they care about. But if you understand their perspective and explain how this can put their other goals at risk, they are more likely to listen and take action.

Why It Matters

Beyond assuming that information alone will inspire stakeholders to address problems, the most common belief I see from technical people is that, if they do excellent work, that work will speak for itself. This could not be further from the truth. Your stakeholder in most cases will not be trained in your technical specialty. Your designs, research, code, or other project work will matter to them only to the degree that you can connect that work to their reality. They will matter only if you show your stakeholder *why* they matter.

This requires extra work to connect the dots in presentations, but that work is well worth the effort.

How to Connect the Dots

Creating an excellent presentation or deliverable is a lot like any research project. You'll start with your goal and work backwards. You'll need to know your audience—hopefully you've built that knowledge already with the skills introduced in the previous chapters! Then frame your intended outcome—what do you want your stakeholders to do or decide based on what you are presenting? Once you have that, it should be reasonably straightforward to articulate the key message they should walk away with. Then you can actually start building the presentation by developing your narrative and determining the presentation format.

Here is the process at a high level:

1. Know your audience.
2. Define your goals.
3. Build a narrative—what is the most important thing for your audience to walk away with?
4. Choose a format.

1. Know Your Audience.

The first step on the list, know your audience, is the work discussed throughout this book already. Who are your stakeholder(s)? What is important to them, and what do they most need to hear?

2. Define Your Goals.

Once you have considered your audience, figure out what you want to present to them. Start with what you want to achieve, and work backwards. For example, if what you want is for the stakeholder to approve your suggested path of work, consider what decision would lead to that path versus another. What outcomes would the stakeholder want from that decision? What actions might need to be taken? How can you make the case that Path A will result in these outcomes?

For example, when I did my work with small businesses, I learned about how the small business lifecycle and the goals of the individual owners impacted their businesses. While I wanted my stakeholders to understand these nuances and complexity, I knew that they would care most about marketing opportunities. I had to make the case that looking at customers only in terms of demographics would equate to missing opportunities to form deeper relationships (and, yes, sell more) to these customers.

"Growth" meant different things to different business owners, and so did the mail.

In the case of a user experience designer, you might want your stakeholder to understand the things they can do to improve the user experience. But you may first need to establish that improving the user experience will deliver their preferred goals. Your stakeholders may care about saving money, bringing in new revenue, or having the quickest path to implementation. So you will use what is important to them to make your case. Think through how to make your argument and support with facts as needed.

You've spent considerable effort to understand your stakeholder, and this moment is when it truly pays off. The most persuasive presentations tell the stakeholder clearly and succinctly how your guidance gives them what they want.

3. Build a Narrative.

Now that you know your argument, you'll need to focus your presentation or deliverable to a clear, single point or argument. I like to use a thought exercise. If you had two minutes to present to a room full of stakeholders, what one thing would you say to them? That is the key message of your presentation or deliverable—the one thing you want them to walk away with, even if they forget (or don't hear) the rest.

Once you have articulated the key message, you can expand your two-minute talk to a longer format. Don't add more key points. Instead, support your main message with subpoints and significant details. Build up the presentation, for example, to five minutes, ten, and then twenty, crafting a longer story based on your main message with additional details. What is the beginning, middle, and end of the story that supports your main argument? Every detail of your presentation or deliverable should support that.

This advice goes counter to many people's natural instinct, which is to start with everything and then edit it down. Unfortunately a presentation with twenty things to say feels like one with nothing to say. How can your stakeholder make meaning out of so much information? A well-crafted narrative lands more clearly and persuades more strongly. It does the work for them, connecting your guidance to their reality.

Unless you have a pressing reason to do otherwise, methods and processes should not be part of the narrative and should instead be relegated to an appendix for those who care.[10] Similarly, don't dump all of your data into the presentation; if you need to provide it, do so in a comprehensible, digestible form, such as in a separate repository. Your presentation should be reserved for the clear *meaning* that comes from the data, not the weight of the data itself.

Of course if you have been specifically told to provide data, you will need to deliver what you have been contracted to deliver. But you can still frame your data into a coherent single story that (1) makes a point and (2) prods into action, even if that action is to recommend focus from the organization.

Storytelling

The way that I use "story" may be different from the usage you have previously heard. A story in a presentation is more than an account of incidents or events; it is a path to understanding.

---

10 I am well aware that some rare stakeholders need to hear about your rigorous methodology before they will give anything else the time of day. Use your listening and relationship-building skills to identify this kind of stakeholder and act accordingly. But don't assume you have to "establish credibility" in this way with every stakeholder. With stakeholders not expressly interested in it, the methodology discussion may actively undermine you.

Narrative is one of the fundamental ways that humans organize, explain, and understand our own experiences. It is also the chief way we are able to move outside our own experience into the experiences of others. Good narrative structure can enable decision makers to both see the import of the data and the path to action.

A cloud of data is noise. A list of isolated topics is structured noise. Story has meaning. When you can tell a story from your data or topics, your audience understands the *meaning*.

Of course the narrative structure I'm discussing doesn't have to involve any anecdotes—it isn't about stringing together accounts of stories that happened to people. Instead, it is a framework that relays what is important. It highlights your key theme to make clear what matters and builds around that key point. A good narrative structure helps you edit out what is extraneous and would distract from the meaning you are building.

Don't make your audience do the work of sensemaking! Instead, use a story to guide the audience down the path gently without, as one of my colleagues puts it, "realizing they are led down the path." You do this by building a series of connections and meanings with a destination they clearly understand.

You do not simply tell the audience that something is interesting, you tell them *why* it is interesting in the context they care about.

Sensemaking

Making a single narrative out of your data is time consuming and difficult. Sensemaking takes effort—and it can literally be the difference between life and death in terms of what is remembered.

Edwin Tufte has argued that seven people died in the Challenger disaster because of a PowerPoint slide. While the engineering team making the presentation (and slide deck) knew there was a potential risk when large pieces of foam hit the shuttle, they had buried this data deep in the presentation without calling out the implications. In fact, the slide that contained the most critical information was wall-to-wall text with a headline that gave a misleading positive spin. The engineers thought that the space shuttle wing tile was likely to be compromised, which could imperil safe re-entry. But they failed to identify that risk clearly or draw the conclusion that the landing should be canceled until maintenance could be done. Decision makers thought that the risks had been analyzed by and deemed unimportant by the engineers. The launch continued as scheduled… and the space shuttle burned up on re-entry.[11]

What would have happened if the engineers had done the sensemaking and explained why the data mattered? They could have explicitly said that there was a risk that had not been sufficiently tested, putting astronauts' lives in danger. With clear context and conclusions, suddenly the decision maker knows they should act.

Consider Your Audience

As you craft your presentation, consider your audience. You want your narrative to bring others along so that they end up at the same destination you have reached. But you should not tell the story of how you personally got to that destination; instead construct the story that will matter most to your audience.

When in doubt, use the framework of your stakeholders that you've worked so hard to understand. Use their preferred method of communication and presentation.

---

11 Thomas, James. 2019. "Death by PowerPoint: The Slide That Killed Seven People." McDreeamie-Musings (blog). April 15, 2019. https://mcdreeamiemusings.com/blog/2019/4/13/gsux1h6bnt8lqjd7w2t2mtvfg81uhx.

Curating a Story

Constructing a story involves curation—a careful and thoughtful process of what details and points to include and what to exclude. Building the narrative involves editing, choosing what to relay to our audience and the meaning to make out of it.

This goes back to the classic research questions that should always be considered: who, what, why, and how:

- **Who** is the audience?
- **What** one thing do you want them to take away from the story?
- **Why** do you want them to take this away?
- **How** are you going to relay the story so that it has the intended effect?
- **What** points, structure, and details support the story without distracting from it?

Some additional principles to create strong stories for your presentations and deliverables:

- **Be direct.** Tell people what you want them to know and what you are recommending clearly and succinctly.
- **Support your conclusions** with data, but don't lead with data.
- **Explain why** the conclusion / recommendation is important and should matter to your stakeholders in terms they care about.

An Example Story

A different year during my time at Pitney Bowes, I did a qualitative evaluation of a new corporate policy designed to limit the delivery of Standard Mail and to stop the delivery of personal mail entirely within the company. (For those who aren't familiar with the company, Pitney Bowes's primary business is related to mail! So the policy was a significant choice.)

The stated aim of the policy was to reduce the environmental impact of the mail and to increase efficiency. So when it came time to present the findings of the research, we had a dilemma. We wanted them to revert the policy since our data showed it was affecting employees negatively. But in order to be heard, we had to frame our data in reference to the things they cared about: environmental impact and efficiency.

We were able to present data that showed neither goal was being met and to describe a few other negative impacts of the policy. But our conclusion was not, "Stop the policy because it is bad," but rather, "Based on our research, here are specific recommendations that we believe will help you better achieve these two desired outcomes."

4. Choose a Format.

How you present will have an impact on how your message is received. What formats are best suited to your audience and outcomes? Sometimes you won't have a choice. For better or for worse, slideshows still seem to be the currency of industry communications. There are also some environments where written reports are expected or even where required templates constrain your ability to frame narratives in the ways described earlier in this chapter. If you do have a choice, however, make it strategically.

Keep in mind that slides and documents are not the only options in terms of artifacts and media. If your stakeholder is best reached through other means, such as audio, video, or other artifacts, you may wish to construct the story of your presentation in a way that takes advantage of the benefits of that format.

Workshops and Working Sessions

People often think about a workshop or a working session as a meeting, twenty people in a room for two hours with an outcome in mind. Decisions are almost never made in the two hours—instead, you have a strong conversation in which people uncover issues and articulate assumptions. You're giving them the time and space to think through hard decisions with others and to reshape assumptions. As such, it's an ideal time to give an informal presentation while you guide and facilitate discussion.

Remember that telling people they are wrong is not the best path to win friends and influence people. When you communicate strategically in a workshop, in a working session, or in other forums, you do the work to ensure your points are heard. You speak in the terms your audience cares about, and that earns you trust.

Accessibility

Is your presentation accessible to your audience? Don't forget that, while storytelling is primarily an oral form, not everyone can hear clearly. Likewise, assuming that images or visuals will relay the story on their own does not take into account visual impairments. Movement and animations can also be challenging for many kinds of cognitive models. When in doubt, consider the needs of your stakeholders and your audience, and do the work to reach them in their best media using their framework.

Artifacts

When you create artifacts, visuals, and other documents, consider whether or not they stand on their own without you there to explain them. That highly complex system map may be powerful in the moment, but it won't be used for decision making later if they can't parse it on their own. Spend the extra time to build artifacts that speak for themselves; you will be successful to the degree you do not make stakeholders do the work of sensemaking.

Messages in Writing

Be aware that anything in writing can be misconstrued; without the tone of voice or body language of face-to-face speech, words can end up coming across very differently to different people. Some forms of writing (email, Slack) are far more subject to misinterpretation than others. Slide decks that are distributed without you being there to explain them can also cause issues. So for important presentations, messages, and documents, it may be worth having a colleague glance over it to make sure it says what you intended.

Meetings Are Presentations Too

Not every presentation is formal. There are many times when I go through all of the steps of preparing for a presentation (except the slides) when I know I'll have to speak up in a meeting. If I'm trying to get someone to make a decision, *how* I present the information to them will make all the difference to whether I can persuade them to my side.

Sometimes you'll need to do the work of preparing a presentation without the slides so that you can express your message with clarity.

How to Apply This Chapter

Now that you know what you want to say to your stakeholder, create your own two-minute presentation.

- What is the most important thing you can communicate to your stakeholder? If there's one thing you want to make sure they walk away with, what is it?
- Now craft a two-minute talk or one-paragraph summary of your point in your stakeholder's language. Use non-technical terms.
- Clearly articulate *why* your point is important. Does it decrease risk or increase profits? Will it prevent the space shuttle from exploding?
- Now create subpoints and details to support your major point.
- Continue to expand your story, curating significant details, until it fits the size of the talk or presentation you will give.
- Finally, go back through the presentation and ensure you're using your stakeholder's language throughout.

Two-Minute Summary

If you present well, you give your stakeholders clear recommendations and a central point to take away. As such, you not only teach your stakeholders how to think about your work, you give them a practical way to use it—delivering impact.

- Designs, research, and data don't speak for themselves. You must make the connection between your technicals and their goals.
- Frame your presentation in terms of your stakeholders' goals and priorities, not yours.
- Pick a single point, and expand that point to a clear narrative.
- Choose the right time and media for your words to make the most impact. Avoid embarrassing anyone.

CHAPTER SEVEN
WHEN STAKEHOLDERS ARE DIFFICULT

Most of the time, working well with seemingly difficult people means changing your behavior. But sometimes the best you can do with a genuinely difficult person is to mitigate the harm.

RECENTLY A WEB DESIGN COLLEAGUE WAS TALKING TO ME about a difficult stakeholder at an outside organization, someone I'll call Martin. This stakeholder was known to be unpredictable and, when giving design and technical feedback, would be imprecise and emotion-driven. He would also get angry if the designers asked too many clarifying questions or if they did not deliver what he had had in his head. What was worse, he was actively insulting to the team. For example, my colleague would present her team's excellent work to the stakeholder, explaining their approach carefully and with a great deal of context, and he would respond with vague, negative words and even unhelpful emojis. (In one notable case, he responded only with a poop emoji her team took very personally.)

Martin's behavior was difficult, and some members of the team chose to interpret it as insulting. Later, my colleague discovered Martin was being bombarded with constant requests both in regards to her team's work and to his internal projects, and all of those projects followed different processes. The deluge would have stressed many people out and make them not behave well—and while this did not excuse his behavior, it started to *explain* it. Understanding the behavior is a first step toward improving the situation.

My colleague responded to this information by considering. How might her team shift their way of working to ameliorate the situation? Could they develop a more consistent process for feedback that also created less emails and interactions that needed immediate attention? The team collaborated with Martin to find a process that decreased the multiple streams of requests and made the work more predictable for him.

The new process for interactions dramatically decreased the amount of negative unconstructive feedback the team received from Martin. While the project still stressed my colleague greatly at times, it was ultimately successful. She and I celebrated when the project ended and she could move on.

Right or wrong, stakeholders have power. They are also frequently overloaded with demands with little energy for non-critical tasks. If you wait for your stakeholder to change, you may end up waiting forever. Instead, take the defensive driving approach, and change your behavior first. Your actions will alter the dynamics of the situation, and if you are lucky, the stakeholder will then choose to change too.

The difficult stakeholder may still be difficult, but in many cases, you can adjust and still bring the project to completion successfully.

Difficult People and Defensive Driving

Dealing with a difficult stakeholder is, in many ways, like defensive driving. You can improve your skills: level up to parallel park, do a tricky three-point turn with a smile, and navigate without a guide. Just like with driving, however, no matter how good you are, you will still have to deal with the consequences of other peoples' actions. You must sometimes drive defensively—take responsibility for the road and problems that aren't your fault in order to avoid an accident and get to your destination successfully. The same is true for dealing with stakeholders; if your stakeholder is difficult, you may not have caused the problem. You can still drive the solution or—in the worst case scenario—conduct yourself in such a way as to mitigate damage.

Many difficult people are predictably and coherently difficult. You can often figure out their motivations, adjust your approach, and get better results from the interaction—that is if you do not throw up your hands and cede control to the other person's actions. Good drivers don't present their cars to be struck squarely by aggressive drivers; they take steps to maintain distance and course correct to be more difficult to hit. Even in the case where your efforts fail, you will tend to suffer less damage if you take this approach.

> **Note:** In the rare cases where your stakeholder is abusive or cruel without reason, sometimes there is nothing you can do to truly fix the relationship. There are still strategies on how to keep the damage from that stakeholder as limited as possible to yourself and your team until you have the opportunity to leave. I will discuss these later in the chapter.

Stakeholder relationships are never entirely within your control, but regardless of the situation, there are things that you can do to improve the situation.

The Environment Can Drive the Behavior

Before we continue, I think it's important to highlight a simple truth about difficult stakeholders: everybody is difficult sometimes. Every person on Earth—including you and me!—is better behaved under some sets of circumstances than others. We can be stressed by a bad day, by unfortunate events in our personal life, or simply by too many things happening at once. But we can also be put into longer-term situations and environments that keep that stress high and affect our behavior for the worse on a daily basis.

To put it simply, some environments bring out the worst in people, and other environments let them access their best selves. That is the point of us making changes in our working style to support stakeholders better. Changing your approach to interacting with a particular person changes the environment. It may de-escalate the situation and, in the process, decrease the emotions driving some of their behavior. This may let your stakeholder's best self emerge into the interaction. It also may not, but it's well worth a try.

The point of the listening practices and small talk I introduced earlier in the book was to establish an environment of trust and collaboration. When your stakeholder trusts you to work on their behalf, most will respond less reactively. The relationship will improve and the environment in which the project is conducted will improve. So if your stakeholder is difficult and you have not yet put in this foundational work, it's worth doing that work again. That step alone may improve your situation.

The rest of this chapter addresses what to do if these listening and relationship-building practices are still failing.

Changing Your Behavior

You should begin your work of improving a relationship with a difficult stakeholder by looking at your own behavior. Are you potentially contributing to the problem? If so, this is good news because you will be able to correct your part of the dynamic quickly.

Here I will pause to ask you to honestly assess your role. Could you be partially or directly at fault in the interaction? Have you been cranky and demanding of your stakeholder? Are you saying no too often? Are you delivering low quality or late work or failing to manage expectations well? Take an honest look at your actions and your team's from the perspective of your stakeholder.

If your actions are otherwise not at fault, consider communication and working style. How often are you communicating with your stakeholder? How many people are communicating with them and at what cadence? Are you framing your communications in the terms they will most easily understand and care about? If you identify a potential driver of the issue, you can solve it. In most cases the stakeholder issue will resolve or lessen in response.

Communication

In the case of Martin, he was being bombarded by more than a dozen designers coming to him for decisions. In the case of another stakeholder in my recent experience, she was getting no visibility into a project, and the silence was leading directly to anxiety. In her case, frequent updates led to more trust, less worry, and less misbehavior. She needed something very different from what Martin needed for a good relationship.

Ask your stakeholder about the frequency and content of your communication. Do they need more or less communication?

Do you need to change to support them better in some other way? They may or may not be able to articulate specific changes without prompting. If not, take a moment to consider the situation from their perspective. How would you perceive your own behavior, given what you know about what's important to them? Are you acting in a way that might be incongruent with their preferred style or goals?

After your conversation with your stakeholder, make changes or suggest them in your own behavior. Again, you may not be the problem, but shifting to better support your stakeholder means you are taking *responsibility* for the solution. This makes it far more likely that the negative behavior will improve on their end, even if partially.

Things to Consider Changing About Communication

Consider what parts of the interaction you might change, using the following categories:

- Frequency of communication
- Communication style (direct or indirect, question or statement-driven inquiry, how much information to give at one time, etc.)
- Your tone of voice and delivery
- The tone of your written communication
- How much detail you give and at what speed
- Framing your communication in terms that matter to them
- When and why they are copied on emails not directly to them
- How often you consult them on decisions and at what level
- The process you are working by (when in doubt, adjust to their approach, with more documentation if needed)

- How you treat the power dynamic
- How you express respect and in what terms

Obviously you cannot control the other pressures that your stakeholder is under. Your influence on their behavior is only partial at best. It is, however, the portion of the equation you can control, and it's always worth starting there. Where can you assess what's working and what you can change or suggest changing? When in doubt, shift your approach to *their* way of working rather than your own.

Outcomes and Presentation

After having mentored many talented individuals over the years, I have identified a few common mistakes that technical people often make beyond communication styles. If you're delivering excellent work on time with a good attitude, but your stakeholder is still unhappy, address potential communication first. Then widen your lens.

If your stakeholder is still unhappy after you adjust your communication style, the most likely problem is that your work is not actually giving the *outcomes* they want.

For example, designers can often focus on creating designs for the best user experience possible at the expense of features or results. These designers see their job as serving the end user one hundred percent of the time. In the earlier story about the user interface for the printer, for example, the designer's focus on the user experience on the touch screen led her to hide the ink reorder button. As beautiful and user-friendly as that work was, it was still fundamentally unsuccessful in adding to the company's bottom line.

The job of every technical professional is to find a happy medium between technically excellent work and delivering the priorities of the stakeholder within the constraints they give you. Otherwise, your technically excellent work becomes useless.

If you are certain that you are delivering outcomes and communicating with the correct tone and frequency, come back to your presentation skills from the last chapter. The stakeholder may not realize your work is delivering their goals!

Take the time to reframe what you have done in their language, making it clear how exactly you have answered their wants and needs within their constraints. **Show them *why* your work matters to them in their terms, and you may find the relationship improves dramatically.** It also might not; stakeholders are individuals, and each will respond in their own way to input.

Can You Change the Process?

When facing a difficult stakeholder, I like to adjust processes where possible with an eye to improving interactions.

Let me walk you through an example of how this might play out. Recently, a junior colleague roped me into a meeting to "change our process because we need the stakeholder to be more accountable." I attended that meeting with a strong word of warning: "We do not hold stakeholders more accountable." That is not how we serve them in this company. (It's a misunderstanding of the power relationship.) That being said, after hearing the details of the situation I agreed with them on one point: the stakeholder, Valerie, was being legitimately difficult. She had changed her mind regularly in ways that cost the team work time, and there was no perfect solution. Yet the team's process was partially to blame.

The team had detailed minutes of every meeting but had not taken the time to establish agreement in writing. When the stakeholder came back with a different answer than they expected, they unfortunately responded, "You agreed. You need to read the minutes." When it happened more than once, a junior team member literally responded that it wasn't fair for Valerie to keep changing her mind.

The instinct to document was a good one, but the approach wasn't helpful. Valerie may not have meant a passing comment in a meeting to be marching orders and was certainly not going to read meeting minutes to investigate the claim that she was contradicting herself. Instead, it would be much easier for the stakeholder (and for the team) to have a decision log with an explicit approval process. A decision log tends to guide everyone to a solid, relatively final decision, and it's easily referenced in future without much legwork. The same goes for risk registers and other similar documentation tools.

Now in this case, Valerie continued to change her mind more than the team would have liked. When the team used a decision log, though, she did so less often and was more conscious of the implications and open to discussion. The team also felt more grounded and less whiplashed by changes.

Optimizing both your process and your environment can help smooth out the relationship with a seemingly difficult stakeholder. For example, if the relationship with your stakeholder is rocky, it may benefit from a change in meeting format. If you are meeting with your stakeholder in a large group of stakeholders or in a meeting of hundreds, try a one-on-one. Alternatively, if the one-on-one format isn't working, try inviting a small number of other stakeholders or experts with direct experience to join a meeting, and see if it shifts the dynamic. Often someone's behavior will change depending on the environment they are in. Another approach to consider is pregaming a meeting, having an earlier meeting with a smaller set of stakeholders in preparation for when you bring the more difficult ones into the room. Sometimes important decisions should be made in smaller groups before adding people to commentate.

Some other approaches to consider are using tools such as risk registers or agendas to focus conversations and decisions or scheduling decision workshops or working sessions with your stakeholder during which they do work or give you needed input. If none of these approaches work, try changing the expectations around meetings and documents based on what you know of your stakeholder's preferred working style, and see what happens. Or try changing the *process* by which work gets done. A change in environment or expectations can make a huge difference in behavior.

Types of Difficult Stakeholders

Now that I've walked you through the general advice on dealing with difficult (but not abusive) stakeholders, let's turn our attention to coping with specific types of difficult people.

> This section is not for abusive interactions. If your stakeholder is being repeatedly cruel to you or consistently acting in ways that are unfit for the workplace, turn forward to the section "How to Mitigate Damage" instead.

I, my colleagues, and the groups we have worked with have encountered a variety of difficult stakeholders. While this list is by no means exhaustive, here are the most common types of difficult stakeholders and techniques to try, which I will then present to you.

The Stakeholder Grasping for Control may feel out of control or out of their depth in the situation, or they may believe strongly in command-and-control management.

The Stakeholder Who Feels Sidelined feels unsteady or insecure about their standing within the project or company.

The Stakeholder Who Is Not Good at What They Do may not understand the broader ecosystem, product, or project. Rather than acknowledging the gaps in their knowledge or skills, they unsuccessfully try to cover them up.

The Stakeholder Overwhelmed by Life may be going through personal or work challenges that you don't know about.

The Nice Stakeholder Who Can't Make Up Their Mind can be particularly tricky. The underlying relationship is often good, but over time you find you are not getting the direction or prioritization you need.

The Stakeholder Who Doesn't Like You - Unfortunately, sometimes stakeholders simply will not like you. Their dislike may stem from something you've done—but it may also come from another source.

There are other flavors of difficult stakeholders and some who may cross types. There are many different reasons why stakeholders may be difficult, and it may be helpful to begin your response with empathy and understanding. Try to see their perspective and understand *why* they may be acting badly. Even if you only understand their perspective in part, that will still help you customize the techniques for dealing with them.

Talk to the Stakeholder

This should be your first approach with any type of difficult stakeholder. When in doubt about how to manage your stakeholder, ask them about the issue in neutral terms, taking responsibility for the gap in understanding. For example, you might say something like this:

> "It feels like we've changed directions a lot [or other neutral observation]. I wonder if I'm just not understanding everything. What can I do?"

or

> "I feel like there's a gap here in our communication. What am I missing? I'm happy to make a change if it would be helpful."

or

> "You seem frustrated by [this]. Please tell me what I should have done differently."

Then use the information you get and your experience of the situation to make interactions easier or clearer for the stakeholder if you can. Try changing your behavior or the process, as described in the story with Valerie and the decision logs above. The *type* of stakeholder is often less important to the solution than the way you yourself approach the problem. Of course, even your best efforts may only *improve* the situation without solving it. That happens to us all.

In addition, here are some specific strategies that you may find help your relationship with certain types of difficult stakeholders. Adapt them to your circumstances and your specific stakeholder.

Let the Stakeholder Be Right

Many stakeholders have a strong need to lead and be right. In these instances, allow them to be right and to direct processes. The skills you learned in the chapter "Saying No Without Saying No" will be particularly important; begin a discussion about priorities or changes by saying that you are committed to giving them what they need and want to clarify things so you can do deliver that outcome. If they've said something wise or correct in the past and it makes sense to bring that up again, do so. You will get further with this stakeholder by praising their past judgment and avoiding the perception that they are being questioned. Know you will need to compromise.

Ask the Stakeholder for Advice

This approach is similar to but distinct from the above. Go to the difficult stakeholder and ask them for advice. A colleague recently resolved a situation with a difficult stakeholder who was always blocking things by asking, "I'm having [this challenge]. What's your advice for how I can do [thing X] better?" The conversation opened up a discussion about the stakeholder's point of view and priorities. It turned out that the stakeholder felt that they were being consulted far too late in the process. That gave my colleague the key to move work forward with a relatively small change to the process regarding timing.

Most people find being asked for advice on an issue to be flattering. It allows them to be the expert teaching you how to do something correctly. If you can stay present and ask good follow-up questions, you can often get the stakeholder to speak at length about issues they may not have brought up before in ways that allow you to act. Keep in mind that you don't have to ask directly about your project for that stakeholder to get benefit from the insight this conversation may provide

Ensure the Stakeholder Feels Heard

Many stakeholders simply need to feel heard, respected, and important. To ensure this, it's critical to build a strong relationship. Take care with actions. Consult with them on decisions, and provide them with all the information they want.

For example, Margot was a key stakeholder on a project my team and I were working on. She was an experienced director of an important department that nonetheless was often deprioritized in internal decisions. Margot had the necessary expertise and experience to weigh in on decisions my team was making, and the official hierarchy supported her position as stakeholder. But she was, in fact, being sidelined by her peers within this conversation. Her response, as of the time our team arrived, was to get loud. She threw wrenches into our work, trying to move the priorities we had been given to the priorities of her specific department.

I couldn't change the organization's priorities, but I could include Margot in discussions and help her voice be heard. So I invited her to working sessions on prioritizing our work with other agency leaders. I started with an explanation of the goals the organization had set us and the purpose of our work in the larger sense. That presentation alone exposed Margot to a depth of information she may not yet have been given and gave her insight into the framework within which our work was occurring. She also had an opportunity to weigh in on where and how we should focus that work.

Margot did not get the majority of what she wanted in the situation, but she did get a voice, and she did get visibility. She felt included and heard, and that ended up making all the difference to how she treated us. There were no more last minute change requests and no more complaints to people higher up in the organization that we were no longer doing our job. She got some of what she wanted included in the high-level roadmap and was able to ask questions of me at will.

Inform the Stakeholder Gently

Stakeholders normally rise to positions of power or influence because they are good at *something*. Occasionally, though, their skills or expertise will not match the position or project they have been put in charge of.

When you are facing a stakeholder who is on this shaky ground, try to work with them as a partner. Provide them with information where needed—perhaps more and simpler information if that is called for—and give them a small number of viable choices that serve their goals. But watch how you share information with a stakeholder you need to support in this way. At no point should you make this person *feel* that they are ignorant. If and when you must share information, do so carefully and without too much extraneous technical detail. (I know this is difficult.) Build up detail from a place of making them feel good. While it can be uncomfortable to be that deferential, for them to accept the new information, they will need to feel safe and respected. Otherwise, they will reject your information entirely and make your job much harder.

Watch for Defensiveness

If your stakeholder is also defensive, be very careful with your words in general. Someone who is already on the defensive will often hear things you do not intend! So be cautious with wording, and in particular avoid any phrases that might appear like placing blame on them. Take care with questions. For instance, ask, "Can you help me understand [this]?" rather than demanding information. You may be able to resolve issues by discussing them in the passive voice or by allowing the stakeholder to blame you or a third party not in the room if you are cautious.

Give Two Choices

We have talked about the prioritization conversation before, but it's important to reiterate here. Difficult people are often overwhelmed, so laying out two clear choices with pros and cons can be helpful. Narrow all of the options down *before* talking to them, and use the two choices as opportunities to present your two best courses of actions. Emphasize the pros and cons in that person's language, using their priorities.

Never present an option you're not comfortable with executing. If desired, though, you can use the pros and cons as a way to guide them towards the choice you think is better. Often an overwhelmed stakeholder will rubber stamp one choice with a minor change or two. Even if they don't, the stakeholder will often respond to two contextualized choices with additional conversation about priorities and values that will make future work easier. You can get input and feedback without necessarily having to explicitly ask what you can do better, and this moves the project forward. Giving two choices, with clear pros and cons, often unsticks the situation.

Get Honest Feedback

Sometimes even people who don't like you can be willing to have an open and honest conversation about the issue. If you can open that conversation, approach it by saying something like this:

> "Hey, I think we have a problem here, and I'd like to help resolve it. What can we do differently? What can I do differently?"

If the issue is likely to be rooted in your behavior, claim that behavior openly. For example, if you've been late on work in the past, acknowledge that:

> "I realize, based on the past, you may not fully trust me to be able to do this on time. What are things I can do to help shift that?"

Find out what you can do to re-establish trust and respect, and do those things consistently. Once you are trusted, the relationship will soften, whether it grows to warmth with time or not.

Even the hardest honest feedback (that isn't abusive) is a gift because it allows you to understand what to change and begins to build trust. When they tell you what they are perceiving, thank them. Then ask, "How do we move forward from this?" It's nearly always possible to move forward in some way, to earn some measure of respect and trust again, whether it's been a week or ten years since you've begun working with this stakeholder.

How to Mitigate the Damage

Not every stakeholder situation is fixable, and not every stakeholder will respond well to your efforts. The world's best defensive driver may still get sideswiped by a car running a red light, and the world's most skilled person at stakeholder management won't be able to make a relationship work with every individual.

Of course truly toxic or abusive people lead to bad situations that *will* cause damage to you and your teams. If you can afford to, leaving the situation may be your best approach. If you can fire the client or leave the job quickly without penalty, consider whether doing so is in your best long-term interest, and if so, take immediate action in that direction.

The following strategies will not prevent all damage, no matter how well that you execute them. However, if, like many of us who must work with difficult stakeholders, you cannot leave until the job is done, read on. Then complete the work as well and as quickly as you can, and leave with honor.

Strategy One: Refuse to Fight

Sometimes the best response to a combative stakeholder is simply not to fight. You're not going to win. Give them what they want—the least bad version of what they want that you can produce—and move on. Refusing to fight about it will take some of your own pain away while you wait to leave.

Strategy Two: Become an Order Taker

Until this chapter, I have been consistently recommending taking on the role of a trusted advisor, building good relationships with your stakeholders. When done correctly, this approach leads to a positive cycle, where your listening leads to trust and trust leads to them listening *to you*. However, when trust has been degraded to the point that it cannot be earned back—even if the actions that broke the trust between, say, two companies were not your fault—you will want to stop offering guidance.

I was once in a situation in which my predecessor made some severe mistakes, and I was brought in with a new team to salvage the project. In many other cases before, I was able to have an open and honest conversation with stakeholders about the previous failures, their new priorities, and how to address their concerns moving forward. Generally stakeholders will give me some amount of time to prove myself and my team before writing anything off, and I have had a good track record of pulling out successful projects on second tries. Unfortunately, in this case the stakeholder had decided that I and my team (despite being new) were just as incompetent as our predecessors. My only move was to do exactly what they told me to do in order to starve them of ammunition to use against me and my team. The next six months were painful for everyone involved, but I was largely able to shield the team, and we did a "good enough" job, good enough to run out the clock for the end of the project.

In addition to taking orders, if you can, take on most or all of the interactions with the stakeholder directly, rather than asking individual contributors to coordinate separately. When one of them needs to present work, go along to the meeting ,and speak up in their place to address any problematic questions.

Strategy Three: Minimize Contact

If you must deal with a toxic or abusive person, limit your contact with that person as much as possible. Starving them of contact is more effective than it sounds; this kind of person often thrives on attention. They are *looking* for a reaction from you, and the larger your reaction, the more they act out. The fewer interactions you have with them, and the less interesting your reactions in those conversations, the less you will become a target.

Strategy Four: Document

It cannot be overstated how important it is, regardless of other strategies you may use, to document *everything*. If someone is genuinely toxic or abusive, the more documentation you have, the more recourse you may have. If you can also document how this behavior affects the business, you will have additional needed leverage. Most people have bosses who will take extensive patterns of toxic behavior badly—and those who do not are still ultimately answerable to HR, the board of directors, the public, or other oversight mechanisms. Even though there are laws against abuse, some forms of abuse don't get to that level. But if you can show a negative impact on the business and the things senior people care about, they are more likely to take action against that person.

In the worst case, when you are ready to leave the position, you can provide your documentation to the company for future reference. You will also have the documentation for your own protection, in case the toxic or abusive person attacks you later. The person with "the receipts" is often the one who prevails.

Returning to Relationship Building

When in doubt, build the relationship. If your stakeholder is not truly abusive or toxic, change your own behavior first. Then, if there is still an issue, try to open up the conversation. See if you can have an honest conversation about what the stakeholder needs and any way that you might be failing them. Brace yourself for unpleasant feedback, and be sure that you do not respond defensively—just listen.

Apologize if you need, and take the opportunity to start again. Don't forget to carry that feedback forward with you into other interactions. Learning about yourself is a crucial element of talking to stakeholders.

Even if it is the stakeholder's fault entirely, you can approach the situation as a defensive driver. There is always something you can do to make it better.

How to Apply This Chapter

Now that you've learned techniques for dealing with difficult stakeholders, consider a difficult stakeholder that you work with. Spend some time trying to see their perspective and to understand what is important to them.

Reflect on your behavior. Are you delivering excellent, on-time work? Are there things you can improve or change about your behavior?

Reflect on the reasons your stakeholder might be difficult. Are any of those reasons things you may be able to influence? Consider the stakeholder at the beginning of the chapter who was overwhelmed with inputs, for example. Decreasing the number of things he was expected to weigh in on improved his behavior. Is there a similar change that you can try?

Reflect on the environment of your interactions? Are there things you can change about the process or circumstance to make things easier? For example, could you try using a decision log or creating working sessions?

Two-Minute Summary

Working with difficult stakeholders is hard. Just like with defensive driving, though, you may have to take responsibility for situations that aren't your fault to get to your destination successfully.

- Examine your own part in the situation.
- Adjust your behavior, communication styles, and processes to better support your stakeholder, and hope it encourages them to improve their part.
- Doublecheck that you are delivering the outcomes your stakeholder needs and presenting your work for the most impact.
- Use decision logs, risk registers, and other documentation methods to encourage consensus and clear decisions.
- Adjust your approach to the specific *type* of difficult stakeholder you face, while managing your own difficult emotions.
- Mitigate the damage of toxic or abusive people by minimizing contact, refusing to fight, taking orders, and documenting the details of your interactions.

CONCLUSION

Understanding your stakeholders' point of view, their values and priorities, allows you to position your work for the most impact.

THE SKILL SET FOR SUCCESSFULLY TALKING TO STAKEHOLDERS IS broadly applicable. We have focused throughout this book on your work context and the particular work relationships that contain power differentials, but the techniques for interacting laid out in this book can be extremely helpful in any social situation. Listening to and understanding the perspective of your child's teacher or a potential friend, for example, open the door to solid connections. Whether or not you agree with someone, when you listen to people and understand them, they are naturally more inclined to listen to you in return. They value your input and extend trust, both of which lead to positive results.

Listening to others on a wider scale also provides great benefits to you. When you listen, you are more open to the world, and you learn more from others. Your relationships with your family, your spouse, and your friends are likely to be more harmonious as others feel heard and are more willing to listen to your perspective in turn. Your assumptions are challenged more often, and you remain more flexible and adaptable to inevitable change.

Every day people talk past each other and make assumptions rather than listening and trying to understand. They become stuck in a black-and-white framework rather than looking for the shades of gray and the nuance. How much better would the world be if they engaged with each other instead? How much good would be done if people listened, understood, and tried to take the other's point of view?

You can use the skills you've learned in this book to cultivate that kind of world. Use your powers to build understanding rather than baseless assumptions. Influence other people towards what you believe is the right approach, but don't stop there. Guide those around you also in how to behave in an inclusive way. Build understanding. Challenge and compromise so that we as people can collaboratively move forward. Use what you know for the broader good in your life and work and in the lives of those around you. The world needs your influence.

Earning Influence

Real influence, at life and at work, is built from trust and the practice of cultivating relationships. People know you and like you. As they build experience with you, as they see that you are working on behalf of them and their interests, they trust you more and more. That history lays the foundation for influence. Stakeholders who trust you and believe that what you're doing is going to help them will gladly allow you a larger place in their world.

Technical people often believe that simply showing intelligence or describing facts will be enough. But decision making rarely comes from a basis in fact; it is built from belief systems and the felt reality of emotions. Telling someone the facts about climate change will rarely make them consider giving up their favorite old truck, for example—to make such a large decision, they will need to *feel* the urgency emotionally. In the same way, if you want your stakeholders to trust you, to advocate for you, and to promote you, facts will not serve the purpose. Instead, you must build solid relationships with good feelings, good work, and an established history of trust. The strategies for communication and relationship-building in this book will help you bridge that gap.

As you apply the lessons of this book, specifically to your stakeholders, don't just listen; listen for the goals and objectives that are shaping what they are trying to do. Ask about the values and priorities that shape how the other person perceives the world and the situation. Take the time to place yourself in your stakeholders' shoes, and see if you can understand how they perceive *you*. Then, and only then, can you work most effectively for their benefit. Only then can you earn the deep trust you will need for the influence and impact you want.

The Right Frame

The secret weapon for a better career (and to some degree a better life) is knowing how to position your work to best appeal to the other person. Technically good work isn't enough by itself. All of the facts lined up in neat rows won't matter if you haven't aligned them into the frame that the stakeholder understands. Does it fit into their priorities? Does it matter to their worldview? Can it be used immediately? Or does it require effort to apply?

Don't make the stakeholder go through extra steps to place that work within their reality or apply it to their problems. They may not do so for whatever reason, and your work will be left on the cutting room floor. On the other hand, if you position your work correctly, your stakeholder can take it and run with it immediately. They can hook it onto their train already in motion and reap the benefits quickly. That is how your work will have the impact you want.

Walking Away from the All or Nothing Mindset

I have occasionally had conversations with technical specialists who object that they do not understand the benefit of seeing things from their stakeholder's point of view, especially when they feel it is important to convince the stakeholder of *their own* point of view. This is a limiting, all-or-nothing mindset. Yes, you will have to compromise to address your stakeholder's goals and perspectives. Occasionally, that will mean that you shift your approach and allow yourself to not be 100% right—but if your work is placed in a drawer and forgotten, is being right really worth it?

By taking this approach, you may need to water down the strength of your arguments or to make your point slowly over time. It is still better to do so, to earn *real* impact and influence that you can then use at need, than to hold to a rigid form of "the right way" and be discounted.

In a company I worked for, we once had to lay off a researcher who couldn't adapt to the research needed in the business world. They were highly successful in academia, where good research is far more detailed, rigorous, and time consuming than business can afford. Objectively, what was now considered quality work was a lower bar—and the researcher truly struggled to create what was, to their mind, lesser work. I never want to discount the reality that technical work must sometimes take a backseat to the stakeholder's goals and values to have the most impact. I would still counsel patience and understanding. Impact and rigor may need to happen over time rather than all at once.

For technical people, compromise can be a hard lesson to learn. But all-or-nothing thinking often ends with nothing, potentially with a side order of offending your stakeholder. If people really don't understand your work or how to apply it to their goals, then you've lost. If you remain in the game, bringing small pieces of your perspective to the table over time, you'll earn attention and trust. You may eventually be able to explain to your stakeholder *why* your perspective is better—if you have patience and address their needs first.

Understanding how the world works and what my stakeholders need creates opportunities for me. I can understand how to frame my work for the impact both I and my stakeholder want it to have. I can find success through even difficult projects.

Focus

Before I review the major concepts of the book, I want to re-emphasize the importance of prioritizing. When it comes to work, the hidden trap for every technical specialist is trying to do too many things at once. What is truly most important for you at this moment? Rather than saying, "It's all important," find a way to identify the single, two-minute summary of what you *must* do next in the project. Your work—and your communication—will fail if you try to say or accomplish twelve things at once. Rather, focus on one thing or two if you absolutely must. It's better to be heard on one or two things than ignored on twelve.

Knowing your stakeholders, their goals, and their priorities should inform this decision.

I am serious about the two-minute summary of your work, both in presentations and in priority decisions, by the way. It's easy to observe complexity or tell someone to read your dissertation; it's much harder to explain your idea in a form that makes sense in two minutes. I see this process as its own intellectual challenge, and one that pays off in my own clarity on what it is I am arguing or trying to accomplish. It allows me to learn and grow as a person, as does listening to others. If I cannot summarize something in two minutes, I know that I need to do more work to understand what it is I am actually doing or saying. It becomes a flag pointing to the need for more focus and clarity in the near future.

A Review

I will now recap the major concepts of the book to help cement your learning. First, identify your stakeholders and the hidden drivers of power and influence that will affect your outcomes. Then become familiar with the larger reality of the business and industry you're working within. Apply that knowledge to your project and to the questions you ask your stakeholders.

What do your stakeholders most want and need? If they do not know or cannot fully articulate their goals and priorities, you may need to help them frame their problem space and prioritize their projects. Try to get them to a two-minute summary of what is most important, and apply that approach to yourself as well.

Once you know what your stakeholders want and need, you are in a position to tailor your work to have the most impact on those wants and needs. Apply your skills to truly leverage a good outcome.

Inevitably you will face a situation where you cannot tell your stakeholder(s) yes. Often, if you handle the conversation carefully, reframing and reprioritizing, you will not have to tell them no. On the rare occasions when you *must* say no, do so with respect and integrity.

Present your work to directly address the stakeholder's language and perspective so that they can listen, understand, and easily act on it. Use the two-minute summary to deliver the most impact, and expand out from there.

Lastly, using your newfound knowledge, you can change your behavior to sweeten relationships with seemingly difficult stakeholders. You can manage the few who remain difficult, and ameliorate the problems that remain to protect your team.

I Am Now a Stakeholder

I approached most of this book from the perspective of someone talking with stakeholders on a daily basis. This is true: I take on other peoples' point of view, have conversations with stakeholders I must please regularly, and help them set clear priorities and make hard trade-offs. This approach creates more impact for my role and my work—and, now that I am in a senior role, that work is less technical. Talking with stakeholders actually becomes even more critical as you move up in an organization.

I am also now a stakeholder for many people who report to me and others within the organization. Being a stakeholder doesn't make this process easier. It doesn't mean that I have the final say in most projects; I myself have other stakeholders to report to and other priorities to balance. It's never over. If anything, the problems become more complex, and the difficult stakeholders more difficult.

Yet I maintain the habit of listening to and learning from other people, not because it provides me with an immediate advantage (though it often does), but because understanding creates opportunities for growth. When I listen to other people—my peers, other stakeholders, and those who report to me—I learn. I expand my understanding, and I'm more able to connect my work into the progress already being made on other fronts. I'm more able to take on new challenges and explain myself to others. It allows me to become a better person who is able to accomplish more.

As a stakeholder, I am particularly interested in listening to the people who are doing work on the ground. My knowledge and expertise is based on what I've done in the past, while they are doing something right now. They may be encountering new problems, new situations, and new approaches I have not yet seen. They may have ideas to improve the organization or the project in astonishing ways, ways that I am always open to hearing. So I caution you not to discount where you are right now; even if you are not (yet) a formal stakeholder, if you approach the stakeholder with respect, your influence can make a huge difference.

Somewhere, there is a stakeholder who is ready to listen to you and eager to apply your work to their problems if you approach them correctly and earn their trust over time.

Time for Action

Now that you've reached the end of the book, what will you need to do next? For example:

- Perhaps you need to reach out to a specific stakeholder for one-on-one time.
- Perhaps you need to discover more about a specific project or business context.
- Maybe you need to talk to a colleague about a strategy to deal with that one difficult stakeholder.
- Possibly you need to finally reach out to have the trade-offs conversation you've been putting off.

Make a list of whatever you need to know or do next. Then go back to the ends of the chapter summaries in this book. Add to your list anything about your present situation that pops out at you for each topic.

Don't be afraid if the resulting total list is long; we all end up with things we cannot know or do yet. Cross out anything you know you cannot do this month, and prioritize what remains. Then go learn or do things (or both).

When in doubt, start with just having a nice chat with your stakeholder.

ACKNOWLEDGEMENTS

No book is the work of a single individual, and this book would absolutely not have been possible without the immense amount of assistance Alex Hughes Capell provided in helping me frame my thoughts, putting the right words on paper, and managing the entire process of putting all the pieces together to get this published. She is a shining star (and you should read her Mindspace books). My early readers gave me honest constructive criticism and feedback that I hope I have incorporated appropriately—many thanks to Carter Baxter, Lauryl Zenobi, Robin Beers, Samantha Gottlieb, and Kate Walton. Dustin Kiskadoon generously allowed me to reference his ideas around the Ethics of Refusal and gave me advice on how to improve how I wrote about saying no. I recommend his book Blood and Lightning which will entrance you into the world of tattoo artists. Jennifer Jennings enabled me to present some of these ideas in tutorials and talks for EPIC, which helped me further shape them for practitioners. I want to thank those attendees too for their engagement and input. Danny Chapman provided graphics. Others who tangibly touched this book included copyeditor Marie Daehn, front cover designer John van der Woude, back cover designer Ami Hendrickson, and layout designer Anton Khodakovsky.

The interactions I have experienced and the people I have learned from throughout my career go well beyond those I will be able to list here—but if you have been part of my journey, thank you for being there.

www.ingramcontent.com/pod-product-compliance
Lightning Source LLC
Chambersburg PA
CBHW061759070526
44586CB00023B/2633